Marion Ames Taggart

Winnetou, the Apache Knight

Marion Ames Taggart

Winnetou, the Apache Knight

ISBN/EAN: 9783741110665

Manufactured in Europe, USA, Canada, Australia, Japa

Cover: Foto ©Andreas Hilbeck / pixelio.de

Manufactured and distributed by brebook publishing software (www.brebook.com)

Marion Ames Taggart

Winnetou, the Apache Knight

WINNETOU, THE APACHE KNIGHT.

COMPANION VOLUME.

THE TREASURE OF NUGGET MOUNTAIN. Edited by Marion Ames Taggart. 12mo, cloth, ... 85 cents.

JACK HILDRETH AMONG THE INDIANS.

WINNETOU,
THE APACHE KNIGHT.

ADAPTED FOR OUR BOYS AND GIRLS FROM C. MAY

BY

MARION AMES TAGGART.

NEW YORK, CINCINNATI, CHICAGO:
BENZIGER BROTHERS,
Printers to the Holy Apostolic See.

CONTENTS.

CHAPTER I.
Toward the Setting Sun, . . .

CHAPTER II.
My First Buffalo, ...

CHAPTER III.
Wild Mustangs and Long-eared Nancy,

CHAPTER IV.
A Grizzly and a Meeting, . . .

CHAPTER V.
The Speech of the Apache Chief, . .

CHAPTER VI.
A Wish and Its Tragic Fulfilment, .

CHAPTER VII.
A Compact with the Kiowas, . . .

CHAPTER VIII.
Sam Hawkins Goes Spying, . . .

CONTENTS.

CHAPTER IX.
Waiting the Onslaught, ... 93

CHAPTER X.
The Capture of Winnetou, ... 103

CHAPTER XI.
A Difference of Opinion, ... 116

CHAPTER XII.
A Duel, and Capture by the Apaches, . . . 128

CHAPTER XIII.
Nursed to Health for a Cruel Fate, . . . 142

CHAPTER XIV.
On Trial for Life, ... 155

CHAPTER XV.
A Swim for Freedom, ... 168

CHAPTER XVI.
Tangua's Punishment, ... 180

CHAPTER XVII.
The End of Rattler, ... 190

CHAPTER XVIII.
Teaching Winnetou, ... 204

CHAPTER XIX.
The Burial of Kleki-Petrah, ... 214

WINNETOU, THE APACHE KNIGHT.

CHAPTER I.

TOWARD THE SETTING SUN.

It is not necessary to say much about myself. First of all because there is not very much to tell of a young fellow of twenty-three, and then because I hope what I have done and seen will be more interesting than I am, for, between you and me, I often find Jack Hildreth a dull kind of person, especially on a rainy day when I have to sit in the house alone with him.

When I was born three other children had preceded me in the world, and my father's dreamy blue eyes saw no way of providing suitably for this superfluous fourth youngster. And then my uncle John came forward and said: "Name the boy after me, and I'll be responsible for his future." Now Uncle John was rich and unmarried, and though my father could never get his mind down to anything more practical than deciphering cuneiform inscriptions, even he saw that this changed the unflattering prospects of his latest-born into unusually smiling ones.

So I became Jack Hildreth *secundus*, and my uncle

nobly fulfilled his part of the contract. He kept me under his own eye, gave me a horse before my legs were long enough to bestride him, nevertheless expecting me to sit him fast, punished me well if I was quarrelsome or domineering with other boys, yet punished me no less surely if when a quarrel was forced upon me I showed the white feather or failed to do my best to whip my enemy.

"Fear God, but fear no man. Never lie, or sneak, or truckle for favor. Never betray a trust. Never be cruel to man or beast. Never inflict pain deliberately, but never be afraid to meet it if you must. Be kind, be honest, be daring. Be a man, and you will be a gentleman." This was my uncle's simple code; and as I get older, and see more of life, I am inclined to think there is none better.

My uncle sent me to the Jesuit college, and I went through as well as I could, because he trusted me to do so. I did not set the college world afire, but I stood fairly in my classes, and was first in athletics, and my old soldier uncle cared for that with ill-concealed pride.

When I left the student's life, and began to look about on real life and wonder where to take hold of it, I was so restless and overflowing with health and strength that I could not settle down to anything, and the fever for life on the plains came upon me. I longed to be off to the wild and woolly West—the wilder and woollier the better—before I assumed the shackles of civilization forever.

"Go if you choose, Jack," my uncle said. "Men are a better study than books, after you've been grounded in the latter. Begin the study in the primer of an aboriginal race, if you like; indeed it may be best. There's plenty of time to decide on your future, for, as you're to be my heir, there's no pressing need of beginning labor."

My uncle had the necessary influence to get me appointed as an engineer with a party which was to survey for a railroad among the mountains of New Mexico and Arizona—a position I was competent to fill, as I had chosen civil engineering as my future profession, and had studied it thoroughly.

I scarcely realized that I was going till I found myself in St. Louis, where I was to meet the scouts of the party, who would take me with them to join the surveyors at the scene of our labors. On the night after my arrival I invited the senior scout, Sam Hawkins, to sup with me, in order that I might make his acquaintance before starting in the morning.

I do not know whether the Wild West Show was unconsciously in my mind, but when Mr. Hawkins appeared at the appointed time I certainly felt disappointed to see him clad in ordinary clothes and not in the picturesque costume of Buffalo Bill, till I reflected that in St. Louis even a famous Indian scout might condescend to look like every-day mortals.

"So you're the young tenderfoot; glad to make your acquaintance, sir," he said, and held out his hand, smiling at me from an extraordinary face covered with a bushy beard of many moons' growth and shadowed by a large nose a trifle awry, above which twinkled a pair of sharp little eyes.

My guest surprised me not a little, after I had responded to his greeting, by hanging his hat on the gas-fixture, and following it with his hair.

"Don't be shocked," he said calmly, seeing, I suppose, that this was unexpected. "You will excuse me, I hope, for the Pawnees have taken my natural locks. It was a mighty queer feeling, but fortunately I was able to stand it. I went to Tacoma and bought myself a new scalp, and it cost me a roll of good dollars. It doesn't matter; the new hair is more convenient than the old, especially on a warm day, for I never could hang my own wig up like that."

He had a way of laughing inwardly, and his shoulders shook as he spoke, though he made no sound.

"Can you shoot?" asked my queer companion suddenly.

"Fairly," I said, not so much, I am afraid, because I was modest as because I wanted to have the fun of letting him find out that I was a crack marksman.

"And ride?"

"If I have to."

"If you have to! Not as well as you shoot, then?"

"Pshaw! what is riding? The mounting is all that is hard; you can hang on somehow if once you're up."

He looked at me to see whether I was joking or in earnest; but I looked innocent, so he said: "There's where you make a mistake. What you should have said is that mounting is hard because you have to do that yourself, while the horse attends to your getting off again."

"The horse won't see to it in my case," I said with

confidence—born of the fact that my kind uncle had accustomed me to clinging to high-strung beasts before I had lost my milk-teeth.

"A kicking broncho is something to try the mettle of a tenderfoot," remarked Hawkins dryly.

I suppose you know what a tenderfoot is. He is one who speaks good English, and wears gloves as if he were used to them. He also has a prejudice in favor of nice handkerchiefs and well-kept finger-nails; he may know a good deal about history, but he is liable to mistake turkey-tracks for bear-prints, and, though he has learned astronomy, he could never find his way by the stars. The tenderfoot sticks his bowie-knife into his belt in such a manner that it runs into his thigh when he bends; and when he builds a fire on the prairie he makes it so big that it flames as high as a tree, yet feels surprised that the Indians notice it. But many a tenderfoot is a daring, strong-bodied and strong-hearted fellow; and though there was no doubt that I was a tenderfoot fast enough, I hoped to convince Sam Hawkins that I had some qualities requisite for success on the plains.

By the time our supper was over there was a very good understanding established between me and the queer little man to whose faithful love I was to owe so much. He was an eccentric fellow, with a pretence of crustiness covering his big, true heart; but it was not hard to read him by the law of contraries, and our mutual liking dated from that night of meeting.

We set out in the early dawn of the following morning, accompanied by the other two scouts, Dick Stone and Will Parker, whom I then saw for the first time, and whom I learned to value only less than Sam as the truest of good comrades. Our journey was as direct and speedy as we could make it to the mountain region of New Mexico, near the Apache Indian reservation, and I was welcomed by my fellow-workers with a cordiality that gave rise to hopes of pleasant relations with them which were never realized. The party consisted of the head engineer, Bancroft, and three men under him. With them were twelve men intended to serve as our protectors, a sort of standing army, and for whom, as hard-working pioneers, I, a new-comer, had considerable respect until I discovered that they were men of the lowest moral standards.

Although I had entered the service only for experience, I was in earnest and did my duty conscientiously; but I soon found out that my colleagues were genuine adventurers, only after money, and caring nothing for their work except as a means of getting it.

Bancroft was the most dishonest of all. He loved his bottle too well and got private supplies for it from Santa Fé, and worked harder with the brandy-flask than with his surveying instruments. Riggs, Marcy, and Wheeler, the three surveyors, emulated Bancroft in this unprofitable pursuit; and as I never touched a drop of liquor, I naturally was the laborer, while the rest alternated between drinking and sleeping off the effects.

It goes without saying that under such circumstances our work did not progress rapidly, and at the end of the glorious autumn and three months of labor we found ourselves with our task still unaccomplished, while the section with which ours was to connect was almost completed. Besides our workmen being such as they were, we had to work in a region infested with Comanches, Kiowas, and Apaches, who objected to a road through their territory, and we had to be constantly on our guard, which made our progress still slower.

Personally my lot was not a bed of roses, for the men disliked me, and called me "tenderfoot" ten times a day, and took a special delight in thwarting my will, especially Rattler, the leader of our so-called guard, and as big a rascal as ever went unhanged. I durst not speak to them in an authoritative manner, but had to manage them as a wise woman manages a tyrannical husband without his perceiving it.

But I had allies in Sam Hawkins and his two companion scouts, Dick Stone and Will Parker. They were friendly to me, and held off from the others, in whom Sam Hawkins especially managed to inspire respect in spite of his droll peculiarities. There was an alliance formed between us silently, which I can best describe as a sort of feudal relation; he had taken me under his protection like a man who did not need to ask if he were understood. I was the "tenderfoot," and he the experienced frontiersman whose words and deeds had to be infallible to me. As often as he had time and opportunity he gave me practical and theoretical instruction in everything necessary to know and do in the Wild West; and though I graduated from the high school later, so to speak, with Winnetou as master, Sam Hawkins was my elementary teacher.

He made me expert with a lasso, and let me practise

with that useful weapon on his own little person and his horse. When I had reached the point of catching them at every throw he was delighted, and cried out: "Good, my young sir! That's fine. But don't be set up with this praise. A teacher must encourage his stupid scholars when they make a little progress. I have taught lots of young frontiersmen, and they all learned much easier and understood me far quicker than you have, but perhaps it's possible that after eight years or so you may not be called a tenderfoot. You can comfort yourself with the thought that sometimes a stupid man gets on as well as or even a little better than a clever one."

He said this as if in sober earnest, and I received it in the same way, knowing well how differently he meant it. We met at a distance from the camp, where we could not be observed. Sam Hawkins would have it so; and when I asked why, he said: "For mercy's sake, hide yourself, sir. You are so awkward that I should be ashamed to have these fellows see you, so that's why I keep you in the shade—that's the only reason; take it to heart."

The consequence was that none of the company suspected that I had any skill in weapons, or special muscular strength—an ignorance that I was glad to foster.

One day I gave Rattler an order; it was some trifling thing, too small for me to remember now, and he would have been willing to carry it out had not his mood been rather uglier than usual.

"Do it yourself," he growled. "You impudent greenhorn, I'll show you I'm as good as you are any day."

"You're drunk," I said, looking him over and turning away.

"I'm drunk, am I?" he replied, glad of a chance to get at me, whom he hated.

"Very drunk, or I'd knock you down," I answered.

Rattler was a big, brawny fellow, and he stepped up in front of me, rolling up his sleeves. "Who, me? Knock *me* down? Well, I guess not, you blower, you kid, you greenhorn—"

He said no more. I hit him square in the face, and he dropped like an ox. Fearing mischief from Rattler's followers, and realizing that now or never was my authority to be established, I drew my pistol, crying: "If one of you puts his hand to a weapon I'll shoot him on the spot." No one stirred. "Take your friend away, and let him sober up, and when he comes to his senses he may be more respectful," I remarked.

As the men obeyed me, Wheeler, the surveyor, whom I thought the best of the lot, stepped from the others and came up to me. "That was a great blow," he said. "Let me congratulate you. I never saw such strength. They'll call you Shatterhand out here."

This seemed to suit little Sam exactly. He threw up his hat, shouting joyously: "Shatterhand! Good! A tenderfoot, and already won a name, and what a name! Shatterhand; Old Shatterhand. It's like Old Firehand, who is a frontiersman as strong as a bear. I tell you, boy, it's great, and you're christened for good and all in the Wild West."

And so I found myself in a new and strange life, and beginning it with a new name, which became as familiar and as dear to me as my own.

CHAPTER II.

MY FIRST BUFFALO.

THREE days after the little disciplining I had given Rattler, Mr. White, the head engineer of the next section, rode over to us to report that their work was finished, and to inquire what our prospects were for making speedy connection. When he set out on his return he invited Sam Hawkins and me to accompany him part of the way through the valley.

We found him a very agreeable companion; and when we came to the point where we were to turn back we shook hands cordially, leaving him with regret. "There's one thing I want to warn you of," Mr. White said in parting. "Look out for redskins."

"Have you seen them?" Sam asked.

"Not them, but their tracks. Now is the time when the wild mustangs and the buffaloes go southward, and the Indians follow in the chase. The Kiowas are all right, for we arranged with them for the road, but the Apaches and Comanches know nothing of it, and we don't dare let them see us. We have finished our part, and are ready to leave this region; hurry up with yours, and do likewise. Remember there's danger, and good-by."

Sam looked gravely after his retreating form, and pointed to a footprint near the spring where we had paused for parting. "He's quite right to warn us of Indians," he said.

"Do you mean this footprint was made by an Indian?"

"Yes, an Indian's moccasin. How does that make you feel?"

"Not at all."

"You must feel or think something."

"What should I think except that an Indian has been here?"

"Not afraid?"

"Not a bit."

"Oh," cried Sam, "you're living up to your name of Shatterhand; but I tell you that Indians are not so easy to shatter; you don't know them."

"But I hope to understand them. They must be like other men, enemies to their enemies, friends to their friends; and as I mean to treat them well, I don't see why I should fear them."

"You'll find out," said Sam, "or you'll be a greenhorn for eternity. You may treat the Indians as you like, and it won't turn out as you expect, for the results don't depend on your will. You'll learn by experience, and I only hope the experience won't cost you your life."

This was not cheering, and for some time we rode through the pleasant autumn air in silence.

Suddenly Sam reined up his horse, and looked ahead earnestly through half-closed lids. "By George," he cried excitedly, "there they are! Actually there they are, the very first ones."

"What ?" I asked. I saw at some distance ahead of us perhaps eighteen or twenty dark forms moving slowly.

"What!" repeated Sam, bouncing up and down in his saddle. "I'd be ashamed to ask such a question; you are indeed a precious greenhorn. Can't you guess, my learned sir, what those things are before your eyes there ?"

"I should take them for deer if I didn't know there were none about here; and though those animals look so small from here, I should say they were larger than deer."

"Deer in this locality! That's a good one! But your other guess is not so bad; they certainly are larger than deer."

"O Sam, they surely can't be buffaloes ?"

"They surely can. Bisons they are, genuine bisons beginning their travels, and the first I have seen. You see Mr. White was right: buffaloes and Indians. We saw only a footprint of the red men, but the buffaloes are there before our eyes in all their strength. What do you say about it ?"

"We must go up to them."

"Sure."

"And study them."

"Study them ? Really study them ?" he asked, glancing at me sidewise in surprise.

"Yes; I never saw a buffalo, and I'd like to watch them."

I felt the interest of a naturalist, which was perfectly incomprehensible to little Sam. He rubbed his hands together, saying: "Watch them, only watch them! Like a child putting his eye to a rabbit's hole to see the little bunnies! O you young tenderfoot, what I must put up with in you! I don't want to watch them or study them, I tell you, but hunt them. They mean meat—meat, do you understand? and such meat! A buffalo-steak is more glorious than ambrosia, or ambrosiana, or whatever you call the stuff the old Greeks fed their gods with. I must have a buffalo if it costs me my life. The wind is towards us; that's good. The sun's on the left, towards the valley, but it's shady on the right, and if we keep in the shade the animals won't see us. Come on."

He looked to see if his gun, "Liddy," as he called it, was all right, and I hastily overhauled my own weapon. Seeing this, Sam held up his horse and asked: "Do you want to take a hand in this?"

"Of course."

"Well, you let that thing alone if you don't want to be trampled to jelly in the next ten minutes. A buffalo isn't a canary bird for a man to take on his finger and let it sing."

"But I will—"

"Be silent, and obey me," he interrupted in a tone he had never used before. "I won't have your life on my conscience, and you would ride into the jaws of certain death. You can do what you please at other times, but now I'll stand no opposition."

Had there not been such a good understanding between us I would have given him a forcible answer; but as it was, I rode after him in the shadow of the hills without speaking, and after a while Sam said in his usual manner: "There are twenty head, as I reckon. Once a thousand or more browsed over the plains. I have seen early herds numbering a thousand and upward. They were the Indians' food, but the white men have taken it from them. The redskin hunted to live, and only killed what he needed. But the white man has ravaged countless herds, like a robber who for very lust of blood keeps on slaying when he is well supplied. It won't be long before there are no buffaloes, and a little longer and there'll be no Indians, God help them! And it's just the same with the herds of horses. There used to be herds of a thousand mustangs, and even more. Now a man is lucky if he sees two together."

We had come within four hundred feet of the buffaloes unobserved, and Hawkins reined in his horse. In the van of the herd was an old bull whose enormous bulk I studied with wonder. He was certainly six feet high and ten long; I did not then know how to estimate the weight of a buffalo, but I should now say that he must have weighed sixteen hundred pounds—an astounding mass of flesh and bone.

"That's the leader," whispered Sam, "the most experienced of the whole crowd. Whoever tackles him had better make his will first. I will take the young cow right back of him. The best place to shoot is behind the shoulder-blade into the heart; indeed it's the only sure place except the eyes, and none but a madman would go up to a buffalo and shoot into his eyes. You stay here, and hide yourself and your horse in the thicket. When they see me they'll run past here; but

MY FIRST BUFFALO.

don't you quit your place unless I come back or call you."

He waited until I had hidden between two bushes, and then rode slowly forward. It seemed to me this took great courage. I had often read how buffaloes were hunted, and knew all about it; but there is a great difference between a printed page and the real thing. To-day I had seen buffaloes for the first time in my life; and though at first I only wished to study them, as I watched Sam I felt an irresistible longing to join in the sport. He was going to shoot a young cow. Pshaw! that, I thought, required no courage; a true man would choose the strongest bull.

My horse was very restless; he, too, had never seen buffaloes before, and he pawed the ground, frightened and so anxious to run that I could scarcely hold him. Would it not be better to let him go, and attack the old bull myself? I debated this question inwardly, divided between desire to go and regard for Sam's command, meantime watching his every movement.

He had approached within a hundred feet of the buffaloes, when he spurred his horse and galloped into the herd, past the mighty bull, up to the cow which he had selected. She pricked up her ears, and started to run. I saw Sam shoot. She staggered, and her head dropped, but I did not know whether or not she fell, for my eyes were chained to another spot.

The great bull, which had been lying down, was getting up, and turned toward Sam Hawkins. What a mighty beast! The thick head with the enormous skull, the broad forehead with its short, strong horns, the neck and breast covered with the coarse mane, made a picture of the greatest possible strength. Yes, it was a marvellous creature, but the sight of him aroused a longing to measure human strength with this power of the plains. Should I or should I not? I could not decide, nor was I sure that my roan would take me towards him; but just then my frightened horse sprang forth from our cover, and I resolved to try, and spurred him towards the bull. He heard me coming, and turned to meet me, lowering his head to receive horse and rider on his horns. I heard Sam cry out something with all his might, but had no time even to glance at him. It was impossible to shoot the buffalo, for in the first place he was not in the right position, and in the second place my horse would not obey me, but for very fear ran straight towards the threatening horns. The buffalo braced his hind legs to toss us, and raised his head with a mighty bellow. Exerting all my strength, I turned my horse a little, and he leaped over the bull, while the horns grazed my leg.

My course lay directly towards a mire in which the buffalo had been sleeping. I saw this, and fortunately drew my feet from the stirrups; my horse slipped and we both fell.

How it all happened so quickly is incomprehensible to me now, but the next moment I stood upright beside the morass, my gun still in my hand. The buffalo turned on the horse, which had also risen quickly, and came on him in ungainly leaps, and this brought his flank under my fire. I took aim. One more bound and the buffalo would reach my horse. I pulled the trigger; he stopped, whether from fear or because he was hit I did not know, but I fired again, two shots in rapid succession. He slowly raised his head, froze my blood with a last awful roar, swayed from side to side, and fell where he stood.

I might have rejoiced over this narrow escape, but I had something else to attend to. I saw Sam Hawkins galloping for dear life across the valley, followed by a steer not much smaller than my bull had been.

When the bison is aroused his speed is as great as that of a horse; he never gives up his object, and shows a courage and perseverance one would not have expected of him. So this steer was pressing the rider hard, and in order to escape him Sam had to make many turns, which so wearied his horse that he could not hold out as long as the buffalo, and it was quite time that help arrived.

I did not stop to see whether or not my bull was dead. I quickly reloaded both chambers of my gun, and ran across the grass towards Sam. He saw me, and turned his horse in my direction. This was a great mistake, for it brought the horse's side towards the steer behind him. I saw him lower his horns, and in an instant horse and rider were tossed in the air, and fell to the ground with a dreadful thud. Sam cried for help as well as he could. I was a good hundred and fifty feet away, but I dared not delay, though the shot would have been surer at shorter range. I aimed at the steer's left shoulder-blade and fired. The buffalo raised his head as if listening, turned slowly, then ran at me with all his might. Luckily for me, his moment of hesitation had given me time to reload, and therefore I was ready for him by the time the beast had made thirty paces towards me. He could no longer run; his steps became slow, but with deep-hanging head and protruding, bloodshot eyes he came nearer and nearer to me, like some awful, unavoidable fate. I knelt down and brought my gun into position. This movement made the buffalo halt and raise his head a little to see me better, thus bringing his eyes just in range of both barrels. I sent one shot into the right, another into the left eye; a quick shudder went through his body, and the beast fell dead.

Springing to my feet, I rushed toward Sam; but it was not necessary, for I saw him approaching.

"Hallo!" I cried, "are you alive?"

"Very much so, only my left hip pains me, or the right; I'm sure I can't tell which."

"And your horse?"

"Done for; he's still alive, but he's torn past help. We'll have to shoot him to put him out of his misery, poor fellow. Is the buffalo dead?"

I was not able to answer this question positively, so we made sure that there was no life in my former foe, and Hawkins said: "He treated me pretty badly, this old brute; a cow would have been gentler, but I suppose you can't expect such an old soldier to be lady-like. Let us go to my poor horse."

We found him in a pitiable condition, torn so that his entrails protruded, and groaning with agony. Sam loaded, and gave the poor creature the shot that ended his suffering, and then he removed the saddle and bridle, saying: "I'll be my own horse, and put these on my back."

"Where will you get another horse?" I asked.

"That's the least of my troubles; I'll find one unless I'm mistaken."

"A mustang?"

"Yes. The buffaloes are here; they've begun travelling southward, and soon we'll see the mustangs, I'm sure of that."

"May I go with you when you catch one?"

"Sure; you'll have to learn to do it. I wonder if that old bull is dead; such Mathusalas are wonderfully tough."

But the beast was dead, as we found on investigation; and as he lay there I realized more fully what a monster he was. Sam looked him over, shook his head, and said: "It is perfectly incredible. Do you know what you are?"

"What?"

"The most reckless man on earth."

"I've never been accused of recklessness before."

"Well, now you know that 'reckless' is the word for you. I forbade you meddling with a buffalo or leaving your hiding-place; but if you were going to disobey me, why didn't you shoot a cow?"

"Because this was more knightly."

"Knightly! Great Scott! This tenderfoot wants to play knight!" He laughed till he had to take hold of the bushes for support, and when he got his breath he cried: "The true frontiersman does what is most expedient, not what's most knightly."

"And I did that, too."

"How do you make that out?"

"That big bull has much more flesh on him than a cow."

Sam looked at me mockingly. "Much more flesh!" he cried. "And this youngster shot a bull for his flesh! Why, boy, this old stager had surely eighteen or twenty years on his head, and his flesh is as hard as leather, while the cow's flesh is fine and tender. All this shows again what a greenhorn you are. Now go get your horse, and we'll load him with all the meat he can carry."

In spite of Sam's mocking me, that night as I stood unobserved in the door of the tent where he and Stone and Parker sat by their fire I heard Sam say: "Yes, sir, he's going to be a genuine Westerner; he's born one. And how strong he is! Yesterday he drew our great ox-cart alone and single-handed. Now to-day I owe him my life. But we won't let him know what we think of him."

"Why not?" asked Parker.

"It might swell his head," replied Sam. "Many a good fellow has been spoiled by praise. I suppose he'll think I'm an ungrateful old curmudgeon, for I never even thanked him for saving my life. But to-morrow I'll give him a treat; I'll take him to catch a mustang, and, no matter what he thinks, I know how to value him."

I crept away, pleased with what I had heard, and touched by the loving tone of my queer friend's voice as he spoke of me.

CHAPTER III.

WILD MUSTANGS AND LONG-EARED NANCY.

THE next morning as I was going to work Sam came to me, saying: "Put down your instruments; we have something on hand more interesting than surveying."

"What is it?"

"You'll see. Get your horse ready; we're going to ride."

"And how about the work?"

"Nonsense! You've done your share. However, I expect to be back by noon, and then you can measure as much as you will."

After arranging with Bancroft for my absence, we started; and as Sam made a mystery of the object of our expedition, I said nothing to show that I suspected what it was.

We went back of the ravine where we were surveying to a stretch of prairie which Sam had pointed out the day before. It was two good miles broad, and surrounded by woody heights, from which flowed a brook irrigating the plain. We rode to the westerly boundary, where the grass was freshest, and here Sam securely tied his horse—his borrowed horse—and let him graze. As he looked about him an expression of satisfaction shone on his rugged face, like sunshine on rocks. "Dismount, sir," he said, "and tie your horse strong; we'll wait here."

"Why tie him so strongly?" I asked, though I knew well.

"Because you might lose him. I have often seen horses go off with such companions."

"Such companions as what?" I asked.

"Try to guess."

"Mustangs?"

"How did you know?"

"I've read that if domestic horses weren't well tied they'd join the wild ones when a herd came along."

"Confound it! you've read so much a man can't get the best of you."

"Do you want to get the best of me?"

"Of course. But look, the mustangs have been here."

"Are those their tracks?"

"Yes; they went through here yesterday. It was a scouting party. Let me tell you that these beasts are uncommonly sharp. They always send out little advance-parties, which have their officers exactly like soldiers, and the commander is the strongest and most experienced horse. They travel in circular formation, stallions outside, mares next them inside, and the foals in the middle, in order that the males may protect the mares and young. I have already shown you how to catch a mustang with a lasso; do you remember? Would you like to capture one?"

"Certainly I would."

"Well, you'll have a chance before noon to-day."

"Thanks, but I don't intend to catch one."

"The dickens you don't! And why not?"

"Because I don't need a horse."

"But a real frontiersman never asks whether he needs a horse or not."

"Now look here, Sam; only yesterday you were speaking of the brutal way the white men, though they do not need meat, kill the buffaloes in masses, depriving the Indians of their food. We agreed that was a crime against beasts and men."

"Assuredly."

"This is a similar case. I should do wrong to rob one of these glorious fellows of his freedom unless I needed a horse."

"That's well said, young man; bravely said. Any man, any Christian worth calling so, would feel thus; but who said anything about robbing him of his freedom? Just put your education in lasso-throwing to the proof, that's all."

"That's a different thing; I'll do that."

"All right; and I'll use one in earnest, for I do need a horse. I've often told you, and now I'll say again: Sit strong in your saddle, control your horse well when you feel the lasso tighten, and pull; for if you don't you'll be unseated, and the mustang will gallop off, taking your horse and lasso with him. Then you'll lose your mount and be, like me, only a common foot-soldier."

He was about to give more advice, but stopped suddenly, and pointed to the northern end of the prairie. There stood a horse, one single, solitary horse. He walked slowly forward, not stopping to graze, turning his head first to one side, then to the other, snuffing the air as he came.

"Do you see?" whispered Sam. "Didn't I tell you they'd come? That's the scout come on ahead to see if all's safe. He's a wise beast! See how he looks in all directions! He won't discover us, though, for we have the wind towards us."

The mustang broke into a trot, running to the right, then to the left, and finally turned and disappeared as we had seen him come.

"Did you see him?" cried Sam admiringly. "How wise he is! An Indian scout could not have done better."

"That's so; I'm surprised at him."

"Now he's gone back to tell his general the air is pure. How we fooled him! They'll all be here shortly. You ride back to the other end of the prairie, and wait there, while I go towards them and hide in the trees. When they come I'll chase them, and they'll fly in your direction; then you show yourself, and they'll turn back towards me. So we'll drive them back and forth till we've picked out the two best horses, and we'll catch them and choose between them. Do you agree?"

"How can you ask? I know nothing of the art of mustang-catching, of which you are past master, and I've nothing to do but follow your directions."

"All right. I have caught mustangs before to-day, and I hope you're not far wrong in calling me a 'master' of that trade. Now let's take our places."

We turned and rode in opposite directions, he northward, I southward to the spot where we had entered the prairie. I got behind some little trees, made one end of the lasso fast, and coiled the other ready for use. The further end of the prairie was so far off that I could not see the mustangs when they first appeared, but after I had been waiting a quarter of an hour I saw what looked like a dark cloud rapidly increasing in size and advancing in my direction. At first it seemed to be made up of objects about as big as sparrows, then they seemed like cats, dogs, calves, and at last I saw them in their own proportions. They were the mustangs in wild gallop, coming towards me. What a sight these lordly beasts were, with their manes flying about their necks, and their tails streaming like plumes in the wind! There were at least three hundred head, and the earth seemed to tremble beneath the pounding of their hoofs. A white stallion led them, a noble creature that any man might be glad to capture, only no prairie hunter would ride a white horse, for he would be too conspicuous to his enemies.

Now was the time to show myself. I came out, and the startled leader sprang back as though an arrow had pierced him. The herd halted; one loud, eager whinny from the white stallion which plainly meant: Wheel, squadron! and the splendid fellow turned, followed by all his companions, and tore back whence they had come. I followed slowly; there was no hurry, for I knew Sam Hawkins would drive them back to me. I wanted to make sure I was right in what I had seen, for in the brief instant the herd had halted it seemed to me that one of them was not a horse, but a mule. The animal that I thought a mule had been in the front ranks, immediately behind the leader, and so seemed not merely to be tolerated by its companions, but to hold honorable rank among them.

Once again the herd came towards me, and I saw that I was not mistaken, but that a mule really was among them, a mule of a delicate light brown color, with dark back-stripe, and which I thought had the biggest head and the longest ears I had ever seen. Mules are more suitable for rough mountain-riding than horses, are surer-footed, and less likely to fall into abysses—a fact worth consideration. To be sure they are obstinate, and I have known a mule be beaten half to death rather than take another step, not because it was overladen or the way was hard, but simply because it would not. It seemed to me that this mule showed more spirit than the horses, and that its eyes gleamed brighter and more intelligently than theirs, and I resolved to capture it. Evidently it had escaped from its former owner and joined the mustangs.

Now once more Sam turned the herd, and we had approached each other till I could see him. The mustangs could no longer run back and forth; they turned to the side, we following them. The herd had divided, and I saw that the mule was with the more important part, still keeping beside the white horse, and proving itself an unusually strong and swift animal. I pursued this band, and Sam seemed to have the same design.

"Get around them; I left, you right," he shouted.

We spurred our horses, and not only kept up with the mustangs, but rode so swiftly that we headed them off from the woods. They began to scatter to all sides like chickens when a hawk swoops down among them; and as we both chased the white stallion and the mule, Sam cried: "You'll always be a greenhorn. Who else would pick out a white horse?"

I answered him, but his loud laugh drowned my reply, and if he thought I was after the white horse it did not much matter. I left the mule to his tender care, and in a moment he had come so near her that he threw the lasso.

The noose encircled the beast's neck, and now Sam had to hold on as he had directed me to do, and throw himself backward to make the lasso hold when it tautened. This he did, but a moment too late; his horse did not obey on the instant, and was thrown by the force of the jerk. Sam flew through the air, and landed on the ground with a thump. The horse shook himself free, and was up and off in a moment, and the mule with him, since the lasso was fast to the saddle-bow.

I hastened to see if Sam was hurt, and found him standing, much shaken, but not otherwise the worse. He said to me in mournful tones: "There go Dick Stone's chestnut and the mule without saying good-by."

"Are you hurt?"

"No. Jump down and give me your horse."

"What for?"

"To catch them, of course. Hurry up."

"Not much; you might turn another somersault, and then both our horses would be gone to the four winds." With these words I put my horse after the mule and Dick's horse. Already they were in trouble, one pulling one way, the other another, and held together by the lasso, so I could easily come up with them. It never entered my head to use my lasso, but I grabbed the one holding them, wound it around my hand, and felt sure the day was won. I drew the noose tighter and tighter, thus easily controlling the mule, and brought her back, together with the horse, in apparent subjection to where Sam stood.

Then I suddenly pulled the noose taut, when the mule lost her breath and fell to the ground.

"Hold on fast till I have the rascal, and then let go," shouted Sam, springing to the side of the prostrate beast. "Now!" he cried.

I let go the lasso, and the mule instantly jumped up, but not before Sam was on her back. She stood motionless a moment in surprise, then rushed from side to side, then stood first on her hind legs, then on her fore legs, and finally jumped into the air with all four bunched together, and her back arched like a cat's. But still little Sam sat fast.

"Don't get near; she's going to try her last hope and run away, but I'll bring her back tamed," shouted Sam.

He proved to be mistaken, however; she only ran a little way, and then deliberately lay down and rolled. This was too much for Sam's ribs; he had to get out of the saddle. I jumped from my horse, seized the lasso, and wound it around some tough roots near at hand. The mule, finding she had no rider, got up and started to run off; but the roots were strong, the noose drew tight, and again the animal fell. Sam had retired to one side, feeling his legs and ribs, and making a face as if he had eaten sauerkraut and marmalade.

"Let the beast go," he said. "I believe nobody can conquer her."

"Well, I guess not," said I. "No animal whose father was no gentleman, but a donkey, is going to shame me. She's got to mind me. Look out."

I unwound the lasso from the bushes, and stood astride the mule, which at once got up, feeling herself freed. Now it was a question of strength of legs, and in this I far surpassed Sam. If a rider presses his beast's ribs with strong knees it causes intense pain. As the mule began to try to throw me as she had Sam, I caught up the lasso, half hanging on the ground, and fastened it tight behind the noose. This I drew whenever she began any of her tricks, and by this means and pressure of the knees I contrived to keep her on all fours.

It was a bitter struggle, strength against strength. I began to sweat from every pore, but the mule was dripping, and foam fell from her lips in great flakes. Her struggles grew more and more feeble, her heavy breathing became short gasps, till at last she gave in altogether, not willingly, but because she was at her last limit, and stood motionless with bulging eyes. I drew long, deep breaths; it seemed to me as if every bone and sinew in my body were broken.

"Heavens! what a man you are!" cried Sam. "You're stronger than the brute! If you could see your face you would be scared; your eyes are staring, your lips are swollen, your cheeks are actually blue."

"I suppose so; that comes of being a tenderfoot who won't be beaten, while his teacher gives in and lets a horse and a mule conquer him."

Sam made a wry face. "Now let up, young fellow. I tell you the best hunter gets whipped sometimes."

"Very likely. How are your ribs and other little bones?"

"I don't know; I'll have to count 'em to find out. That's a fine beast you have under you there."

"She is indeed. See how patiently she stands; one feels sorry for her. Shall we saddle and bridle her and go back?"

The poor mule stood quiet, trembling in every limb; nor did she try to resist when we put saddle and bridle on her, but obeyed the bit like a well-broken horse. "She's had a master before," said Sam. "I'm going to call her Nancy, for I once had a mule by that name, and it's too much trouble to get used to another. And I'm going to ask you to do me a favor."

"Gladly; what is it?"

"Don't tell at the camp what has happened this morning, for they'd have nine days' sport with me."

"Of course I won't; you're my teacher and friend, so I'll keep your secrets."

His queer face lighted up with pleasure. "Yes, I'm your friend, and if I knew you had a little liking for me, my old heart would be warmed and rejoiced."

I stretched out my hand to him, surprised and touched. "I can easily give you that pleasure, dear Sam," I said. "You may be sure I honestly care for you with real respect and affection."

He shook my hand, looking so delighted that even my young self-sufficiency could perceive how lonely this rough, cranky old frontiersman was, and how great was his yearning for human sympathy.

I fastened Dick Stone's horse with the lasso, and mounting mine, as Sam got on Nancy, we rode away.

"She's been educated, this new Nancy, in a very good school," Sam remarked presently. "I see at every step she is going to be all right, and is regaining the old knowledge which she had forgotten among the mustangs. I hope she has not only temperament but character."

"We've had two good days, Sam," I said.

"Bad ones for me, except in getting Nancy; and bad for you, too, in one way, but mighty honorable."

"Oh, I've done nothing; I came West to get experience. I hope to have a chance at other sport."

"Well, I hope it will come more easily; yesterday your life hung by a hair. You risked too much. Never forget you're a greenhorn tenderfoot. The idea of creeping up to shoot a buffalo in the eye! Did ever any one hear the like? But though hunting buffaloes is dangerous, bear-hunting is far more so."

"Black bear?"

"Nonsense! The grizzly. You've read of him?"

"Yes."

"Well, be glad you don't know him outside of books; and take care you don't, for you might have a chance to meet him. He sometimes comes about such places as this, following the rivers even as far as the prairie. I'll tell you more of him another time; here we are at the camp."

"A mule, a mule! Where did you get her, Hawkins?" cried all the men.

"By special delivery from Washington, for a ten-cent stamp. Would you like to see the envelope?" asked Sam, dismounting.

Though they were curious, none asked further questions, for, like the beast he had captured, when Sam wouldn't he wouldn't, and that was the end of it.

CHAPTER IV.

A GRIZZLY AND A MEETING.

THE morning after Sam and I had caught Miss Nancy we moved our camp onward to begin labor on the next section of the road. Hawkins, Stone, and Parker did not help in this, for Sam was anxious to experiment further with Nancy's education, and the other two accompanied him to the prairie, where they had sufficient room to carry out this purpose. We surveyors transferred our instruments ourselves, helped by one of Rattler's men, while Rattler himself loafed around doing nothing.

We came to the spot where I had killed the two buffaloes, and to my surprise I saw that the body of the old bull was gone, leaving a broad trail of crushed grass that led to the adjoining thicket.

"I thought you had made sure both bulls were dead," Rattler exclaimed. "The big one must have had some life in him."

"Think so?" I asked.

"Of course, unless you think a dead buffalo can take himself off."

"Must he have taken himself off? Perhaps it was done for him."

"Yes, but who did it?"

"Possibly Indians; we saw an Indian's footprint over yonder."

"You don't say! How well a greenhorn can explain things!" sneered Rattler. "If it was done by Indians, where do you think they came from? Dropped from the skies? Because if they came from anywhere else we'd see their tracks. No, there was life in that buffalo, and he crawled into the thicket, where he must have died. I'm going to look for him."

He started off, followed by his men. He may have expected me to go, too, but it was far from my thoughts, for I did not like the way he had spoken. I wanted to work, and did not care a button what had become of the old bull. So I went back to my employment, and had only just taken up the measuring-rod, when a cry of horror rang from the thicket, two, three shots echoed, and then I heard Rattler cry: "Up the tree, quick! up the tree, or you're lost! he can't climb."

Who could not climb? One of Rattler's men burst out of the thicket, writhing like one in mortal agony.

"What is it? What's happened?" I shouted.

"A bear, a tremendous grizzly bear!" he gasped, as I ran up to him.

And within the thicket an agonized voice cried: "Help, help! He's got me!" in the tone of a man who saw the jaws of death yawning before him.

Evidently the man was in extreme danger, and must be helped quickly, but how? I had left my gun in the tent, for in working it hindered me; nor was this an oversight, since we surveyors had the frontiersmen purposely to guard us at our work. If I went to the tent to get the gun, the bear would have torn the man to shreds before I could get back; I must go to him as I was with a knife and two revolvers stuck in my belt, and what were these against a grizzly bear?

The grizzly is a near relation of the extinct cave-bear, and really belongs more to primeval days than to the present. It grows to a great size, and its strength is such that it can easily carry off a deer, a colt, or a young buffalo cow in its jaws. The Indians hold the killing of a grizzly a brilliant feat, because of its absolute fearlessness and inexhaustible endurance.

So it was to meet such a foe that I sprang into the thicket. The trail led further within, where the trees began, and where the bear had dragged the buffalo. It was a dreadful moment. Behind me I could hear the voices of the engineers; before me were the frontiersmen screaming, and between them and me, in indescribable agony, was their companion whom the bear had seized.

I pushed further in, and heard the voice of the bear; for, though this mighty beast differs from others of the bear family in not growling, when in pain or anger it utters something like a loud, harsh breathing and grunting.

And now I was on the scene. Before me lay the torn body of the buffalo, to right and left were the men, who were comparatively safe, having taken to the trees, which a grizzly bear seldom has been known to climb, if ever. One of the men had tried to get up a tree like the others, but had been overtaken by the bear. He hung by both arms hooked to the lowest limb, while the grizzly reached up and held him fast with its fore paws around the lower part of his body.

The man was almost dead; his case was hopeless. I could not help him, and no one could have blamed me if I had gone away and saved myself. But the desperation of the moment seemed to impel me onward. I snatched up a discarded gun, only to find it already emptied. Taking it by the muzzle I sprang over the buffalo, and dealt the bear a blow on the skull with all my might. The gun shattered like glass in my hand; even a blow with a battle-axe would have no effect on such a skull; but I had the satisfaction of distracting the grizzly's attention from its victim.

It turned its head toward me, not quickly, like a wild beast of the feline or canine family, but slowly, as if wondering at my stupidity. It seemed to measure me with its little eyes, deciding between going at me or sticking to its victim; and to this slight hesitation I owe my life, for in that instant the only possible way to save myself came to me. I drew a revolver, sprang directly at the bear, and shot it, once, twice, thrice, straight in the eyes, as I had the buffalo.

Of course this was rapidly done, and at once I jumped to one side, and stood still with my knife drawn. Had I remained where I was, my life would have paid for my rashness, for the blinded beast turned quickly from the tree, and threw itself on the spot where I had stood a moment before. I was not there, and the bear sought me with angry mutterings and heavy breathing. It wheeled around like a mad thing, hugged itself, rose on its hind legs, reaching and springing all around to find me, but fortunately I was out of reach. Its sense of smell would have guided it to me, but it was mad with rage and pain, and this prevented its instinct from serving it.

At last it turned its attention more to its misfortune than to him who had caused it. It sat down, and with sobs and gnashing of teeth laid its fore paws over its eyes. I was sorry that necessity for saving human life was causing the big fellow such pain, and, with pity for it, as well as desire for my own safety, tried to make it short. Quickly I stood beside it and stabbed it twice between the ribs. Instantly it grabbed for me, but once more I sprang out of the way. I had not pierced its heart, and it began seeking me with redoubled fury. This continued for fully ten minutes. It had lost a great deal of blood, and evidently was dying; it sat down again to mourn its poor lost eyes. This gave me a chance for two rapidly repeated knife-thrusts, and this time I aimed better; it sank forward, as again I sprang aloof, made a feeble step to one side, then back, tried to rise, but had not sufficient strength, swayed back and forth in trying to get on its feet, and then stretched out and was still.

"Thank God!" cried Rattler from his tree, "the beast is dead. That was a close call we had."

"I don't see that it was a close call for you," I replied. "You took good care of your own safety. Now you can come down."

"Not yet; you make sure it's truly dead."

"It is dead."

"You don't know; you haven't an idea how tough such a creature is. Go examine it."

"If you doubt me, examine it yourself; you're an experienced frontiersman, and I'm a tenderfoot, you know."

So saying I turned to his comrade, who still hung on the tree in an awful plight. His face was torn, and his wide-open eyes were glassy, the flesh was stripped from the bones of his legs, and he was partly disembowelled. I conquered the horror of the sight enough to say: "Let go, my poor fellow; I will take you down." He did not answer, or show any sign of having heard me, and I called his comrades to help me. Only after I had made sure the bear was dead would the courageous gang come down from their trees, when we gently removed the wounded man. This required strength to accomplish, for his arms had wound tightly around the tree, and stiffened there: he was dead.

This horrible end did not seem to affect his companions in the least, for they turned from him to the bear, and their leader said: "Now things are reversed; the bear meant to eat us, but we will eat it. Quick, you fellows, take its pelt, and let us get at the paws and steak."

He drew his knife and knelt down to carry out his words, but I checked him. "It would have been more fitting if you had used your knife when it was alive. Now it's too late; don't give yourself the trouble."

"What!" he cried. "Do you mean to hinder me?"

"Most emphatically I do, Mr. Rattler."

"By what right?"

"By the most indisputable right. I killed that bear."

"That's not so. Maybe you think a greenhorn can kill a grizzly with a knife! As soon as we saw it we shot it."

"And immediately got up a tree! Yes, that's very true."

"You bet it's true, and our shots killed it, not the two little needle-pricks of your knife. The bear is ours, and we'll do with it what we like. Understand?"

He started to work again, but I said coolly: "Stop this minute, Rattler. I'll teach you to respect my words; do *you* understand?" And as he bent forward to stick the knife into the bear's hide I put both arms around his hips and, raising him, threw him against the next tree so hard that it cracked. I was too angry just then to care whether he or the tree broke, and as he flew across the space I drew my second and unused revolver, to be ready for the next move.

He got up, looked at me with eyes blazing with rage, drew his knife, and cried: "You shall pay for this. You knocked me down once before; I'll see it doesn't happen a third time." He made a step towards me, but I covered him with my pistol, saying: "One step more and you'll have a bullet in your head. Drop that knife. When I say 'three' I'll shoot you if you still hold it. Now: One, two—" He held the knife tight, and I should have shot him, not in the head, but in the hand, for he had to learn to respect me; but luckily I did not get so far, for at this moment a loud voice cried: "Men, are you mad? What reason have the whites to tear out one another's eyes? Stop!"

We looked in the direction whence the voice came, and saw a man appearing from behind the trees. He was small, thin, and hunchbacked, clad and armed like a red man. One could not tell whether he was an Indian or a white; his sharp-cut features indicated the former, while the tint of his face, although sunburned, was that of a white man. He was bareheaded, and his dark hair hung to his shoulders. He wore leather trousers, a hunting-shirt of the same material, and moccasins, and was armed with a knife and gun. His eyes shone with unusual intelligence, and there was nothing ridiculous in his deformity. Indeed, none but stupid and brutal men ever laugh at bodily defects; but Rattler was of this class, for as soon as he looked at the new-comer he cried:

"Hallo! What kind of a freak comes here? Do such queer things grow in the big West?"

The stranger looked at him calmly, and answered quietly: "Thank God that your limbs are sound. It is by the heart and soul that men are judged, and I should not fear a comparison with you in those respects."

He made a gesture of contempt, and turned to me, saying: "You are strong, young sir; it is not every one can send a man flying through the air as you did just now; it was wonderful to see." Then touching the grizzly with his foot, he added: "And this is the game we wanted, but we came too late. We discovered its tracks yesterday, and followed over hill and dale,

A GRIZZLY AND A MEETING. 47

through thick and thin, only to find the work done when we came up with it."

"You speak in the plural; are you not alone?" I asked.

"No; I have two companions with me. But before I tell you who they are, will you introduce yourselves? You know one cannot be too cautious here, where we meet more bad men than good ones." He glanced significantly at Rattler and his followers, but instantly added in a friendly tone: "However, one can tell a gentleman that can be trusted. I heard the last part of your discussion, and know pretty well where I stand."

"We are surveyors, sir," I explained. "We are locating a railroad to go through here."

"Surveyors! Have you purchased the right to build your road?"

His face became stern as he asked the question, for which he seemed to have some reason; so I replied: "I have occupied myself with my task, and never thought of asking."

"Ah, yes; but you must know where you are. Consider: these lands whereon we stand are the property of the Indians; they belong to the Apaches of the Mascaleros tribe. I am sure, if you are sent to survey, the ground is being marked out by the whites for some one else."

"What is that to you?" Rattler cried. "Don't bother yourself with the affairs of others. Any one can see you are a white man."

"I am an Apache, one of the Mascaleros," the stranger said quietly. "I am Kleki-Petrah."

This name in the Apache tongue is equivalent to

White Father, and Rattler seemed to have heard it before. He bowed with mock deference, and said: " Ah, Kleki-Petrah, the venerated school-master of the Apaches! It's a pity you are deformed, for it must annoy you to be laughed at by the braves."

" They never do that, sir. Well-bred people are not amused by such things, and the braves are gentlemen. Since I know who you are and why you are here, I will tell you who my companions are, or perhaps you had better meet them."

He called in the Indian tongue, and two extraordinarily interesting figures appeared, and came slowly towards us. They were Indians, father and son, as one could see at the first glance. The elder was a little above medium height, very strongly built. His air was truly noble; his earnest face was of pure Indian type, but not so sharp and keen as that of most red men. His eyes had a calm, gentle expression, like one much given to contemplation. His head was bare, his hair worn in a knot in which was stuck an eagle's feather, the badge of chieftainship. His dress consisted of moccasins, leather leggings, and hunting-jacket, very simple and unadorned. From his belt, in which a knife was thrust, hung all the appointments necessary to a dweller on the plains. A medicine-charm with sacred inscriptions cut around its face hung from his neck, and in his hand he carried a double-barrelled gun, the handle adorned with silver nails.

The younger man was clad like his father, except that his garments were showier; his leggings were beautifully fringed, and his hunting-shirt was embellished with scarlet needlework. He also wore a medicine-charm around his neck, and a calumet; like his father he was armed with a knife and a double-barrelled gun. He, too, was bareheaded, his hair bound in a knot, but without the feather; it was so long that the end below the knot fell thick and heavy on his shoulders, and many a fine lady might have coveted it. His face was even nobler than his father's, its color a light brown with a touch of bronze. He seemed to be, as I afterwards learned he was, of the same age as myself, and his appearance made as profound an impression on me then, when I saw him first, as his character has left upon me to-day, after our long friendship.

We looked at one another long and searchingly, and I thought I saw for a moment in his earnest, dark eyes a friendly light gleam upon me.

"These are my friends and companions," said Kleki-Petrah, introducing first the father, then the son. "This is Intschu-Tschuna [*Good Sun*], the chief of the Mascaleros, whom all Apaches acknowledge as their head. And here stands his son Winnetou, who already in his youth has accomplished more deeds of renown than any ten old warriors have in all their lives. His name will be known and honored as far as the prairies and Rockies extend."

This sounded like exaggeration, but later I found that he had spoken only the truth.

Rattler laughed insultingly, and said: "So young a fellow, and committed such deeds? I say *committed* purposely, for every one knows they are only deeds of robbery and cruelty. The red men steal from every one."

This was an outrageous insult, but the Indians acted as though they had not heard it. Stooping down over the bear, Kleki-Petrah admired it, calling Winnetou's attention to its size and strength. "It was killed by a knife and not a bullet," he said as he rose.

Evidently, I thought, he had heard the dispute and wished me to have justice.

"What does a school-master know of bear-hunting?" said Rattler. "When we take the skin off we can see what killed him. I won't be robbed of my rights by a greenhorn."

Then Winnetou bent down, touched the bloody wound, and asked me in good English: "Who stabbed the beast?"

"I did," I replied.

"Why did not my young white brother shoot him?"

"Because I had no gun with me."

"Yet here are guns."

"They are not mine; they were thrown away by these men when they climbed the trees shrieking with terror."

"Ugh! the low cowards and dogs, to fly like tissue-paper! A man should make resistance, for if he has courage he may conquer the strongest brute. My young white brother has such courage."

"My son speaks truly," added the father in as perfect English. "This brave young pale-face is no longer a greenhorn. He who kills a grizzly in this manner is a hero; and he who does it to save those who climb trees deserves thanks, not insults. Let us go to visit the pale-faces that have come into our dominion."

They were but three, and did not know how many we numbered, but that never occurred to them. With slow and dignified strides they went out of the thicket, we following.

Then for the first time Intschu-Tschuna saw the surveying instruments standing as we had left them, and, stopping suddenly, he turned to me, demanding: " What is this ? Are the pale-faces measuring the land ? "

" Yes," I answered.

" Why ? "

" For a railroad."

His eyes lost their calmness, and he asked sternly: " Do you obey these people, and measure with them ? "

" Yes."

" And are paid for it ? "

" Yes."

He threw a scornful glance upon me, and in a contemptuous tone he said to Kleki-Petrah: " Your teachings sound well, but they do not often agree with what I see. Christians deceive and rob the Indians. Here is a young pale-face with a brave heart, open face, honorable eyes, and when I ask what he does here he tells me he has come to steal our land. The faces of the white men are good and bad, but inside they are all alike."

To be honest, his words filled me with shame. Could I well be proud of my share in this matter—I, a Catholic, who had been taught so early: " Thou shalt not covet thy neighbor's goods " ? I blushed for my race and for myself before this fine savage; and before I could rally enough even to try to reply, the head engineer, who had been watching us through a hole in the tent, came forth to meet us, and my thoughts were diverted by what then took place.

CHAPTER V.

THE SPEECH OF THE APACHE CHIEF.

The first question the head engineer asked as we came up, although he was surprised to see the Indians with us, was what had become of the bear.

Rattler instantly replied: " We've shot him, and we'll have bear-paws for dinner, and bear-steak to-night for supper."

Our three guests looked at me as if to see whether I would let this pass, and I said: " I claim to have stabbed the bear. Here are three witnesses who have corroborated my statement; but we'll wait till Hawkins, Stone, and Parker come, and they will give their opinion, by which we will be guided. Till then the bear must lie untouched."

"Not much will I leave it to the scouts," growled Rattler. "I'll go with my men and cut up the bear, and whoever tries to hinder us will be driven off with a dozen shots in his body."

"Hold on, Mr. Rattler," said I. "I'm not as much afraid of your shots as you were of the bear. You won't drive me up a tree with your threats. I recommend you to bury your dead comrade; I would not leave him lying thus."

"Is some one dead?" asked Bancroft, startled.

"Yes, Rollins," Rattler replied. "The poor fellow had jumped for a tree, like the rest of us, and would have been all right, but this greenhorn came up, excited the bear, and it tore Rollins horribly."

I stood speechless with amazement that he should dare go so far. It was impossible to endure such lying, and in my very presence. I turned on Rattler and demanded: "Do you mean to say Rollins was escaping, and I prevented it?"

"Yes," he nodded, drawing his revolver.

"And I say the bear had seized him before I came."

"That's a lie," said Rattler.

"Very well; here's a truth for you," and with these words I knocked his revolver from his hand with my left, and with the right gave him such a blow on the ear that he staggered six or eight feet away, and fell flat on the ground.

He sprang up, drew his knife, and came at me raging like a wild beast. I parried the knife-thrust with my left hand, and with my right laid him senseless at my feet.

"Ugh! ugh!" grunted Intschu-Tschuna, surprised into admiration, which his race rarely betray.

"That was Shatterhand again," said Wheeler, the surveyor.

I kept my eye on Rattler's comrades; they were angry, but no one dared attack me, and though they muttered among themselves they did no more.

"You must send Rattler away, Mr. Bancroft," I said. "I have done nothing to him, yet he constantly seeks a quarrel with me. I am afraid he'll make serious trouble in the camp. Send him away, or, if you prefer, I'll go myself."

"Oh, things aren't as bad as that," said Bancroft easily.

"Yes, they are, just as bad as that. Here are his knife and revolver; don't let him have them, for I warn you they'd not be in good hands."

Just as I spoke these words our three scouts joined us, and having heard the story of Rattler's lying claim, and my counter-statement, they set off at once to examine the bear's carcass to settle the dispute. They returned in a short time, and as soon as he was within hailing distance Sam called out: "What idiocy it was to shoot a grizzly and then run! If a man doesn't intend making a fight, then what on earth does he shoot for? Why doesn't he leave the bear in peace? You can't treat grizzlies like poodle-dogs. Poor Rollins paid dear for it, though. Now, who killed that bear, did you say?"

"I did," cried Rattler, who had come to. "I killed him with my gun."

"Well, that agrees; that's all right. The bear was shot."

"Do you hear that, men? Sam Hawkins has decided for me," cried Rattler triumphantly.

"Yes, for you," said Sam. "You shot him, and took off the tip of his ear, and such a loss naturally ended the grizzly, ha! ha! ha! If you shot again it went wide of the mark, for there's no other gun-shot on him. But there are four true knife-thrusts, two above the heart and two in it; who gave him those?"

"I did," I said.

THE SPEECH OF THE APACHE CHIEF. 55

"You alone?"

"No one else."

"Then the bear belongs to you. That is, the pelt is yours; the flesh belongs to all, but you have the right to divide it. This is the custom of the West. Have you anything to say, Mr. Rattler?"

Rattler growled something that condemned us to a much warmer climate, and turned sullenly to the wagon where the liquor was stored. I saw him pour down glass after glass, and knew he would drink till he could drink no more.

The Indians had listened to our discussion, and watched us in silent interest; but now, our affairs being settled, the chief, Intschu-Tschuna, turned to the head engineer, saying: "My ear has told me that among these pale-faces you are chief; is this so?"

"Yes," Bancroft replied.

"Then I have something to say to you."

"What is it?"

"You shall hear. But you are standing, and men should sit in conference."

"Will you be our guest?" asked Bancroft.

"No, for it is impossible. How can I be your guest when you are on my lands, in my forests, my valleys, my prairies? Let the white men be seated."

"Tell me what you wish of me," said Bancroft.

"It is not a wish, but a command," answered Intschu-Tschuna proudly.

"We will take no command," responded the head engineer with equal pride.

A look of anger passed over the chief's face, but he

controlled himself, and said mildly: "My white brother will answer me one question truthfully. Have you a house?"

"Yes."

"With a garden?"

"Yes."

"If a neighbor would cut a path through that garden would my brother submit to it?"

"No."

"The lands beyond the Rocky Mountains and east of the Mississippi belong to the pale-faces. What would they say if the Indians came to build a railroad there?"

"They would drive them away."

"My white brother has answered truly. But the pale-faces come here on these lands of ours, and drive away our mustangs and kill our buffaloes; they seek among us for gold and precious stones, and now they will build a long, long road on which their fire-horses can run. Then more pale-faces will follow this road, and settle among us, and take the little we have left us. What are we to say to this?"

Bancroft was silent.

"Have we fewer rights than they? You call yourselves Christians, and speak of love, yet you say: We can rob and cheat you, but you must be honest with us. Is that love? You say your God is the Good Father of all men, red and white. Is He only our stepfather, and are you His own sons? Did not all the land belong to the red man? It has been taken from us, and what have we instead? Misery, misery, misery. You drive us ever farther and farther back, and press us closer and closer together, and in a little time we shall be suffocated. Why do you do this? Is it because you have not room enough? No, for there is room in your lands still for many, many millions. Each of your tribes can have a whole State, but the red man, the true owner, may not have a place to lay his head. Kleki-Petrah, who sits here before me, has taught me your Holy Book. There it says that the first man had two sons, and one killed the other, and his blood cried to Heaven. How is it with the two brothers, the red and the white? Are you not Cain, and are we not Abel, whose blood cries to Heaven? And when you try to destroy us you wish us to make no defence. But we will defend ourselves, we will defend ourselves. We have been driven from place to place, ever farther away; now we abide here, where we believed ourselves at rest, but you come to build your railroad. Have we not the same rights you have over your house and garden? If we followed our own laws we should kill you; but we only wish your laws to be fulfilled towards us: are they? No! Your laws have two faces, and you turn them to us as it suits your advantage. Have you asked our permission to build this road?"

"No," said Bancroft. "It was not necessary."

"Have you bought the land, or have we sold it?"

"Not to me."

"Nor to any other. Were you an honest man sent here to build a way for the fire-horse, you would first have asked the man who sent you whether he had a right to do this thing, and made him prove it. But this you have not done. I forbid you to measure further."

These last words were spoken in a tone of most bitter earnest.

I had read much of the red man, but never had found in any book such a speech from an Indian, and I wondered if he owed his fluent English and forcible logic to Kleki-Petrah.

The head engineer found himself in an awkward predicament. If he was honest and sincere he could not gainsay what Intschu-Tschuna had spoken; but there were considerations more weighty with Bancroft than honesty, so the chief had to wait his answer, looking him straight in the eyes.

Seeing that Bancroft was shifting about in his mind for a way out of his difficulty, Intschu-Tschuna rose, saying decidedly: "There is no need of further speech. I have spoken. My will is that you leave here to-day, and go back whence you came. Decide whether you will obey or not. I will now depart with my son Winnetou, and will return at the end of that time which the palefaces call an hour, when you will give me your answer. If you go, we are brothers; if you stay, it shall be deadly enmity between you and me. I am Intschu-Tschuna, the chief of all the Apaches. I have spoken."

Winnetou followed him as he went out from among us, and they were soon lost to sight down the valley.

Kleki-Petrah remained seated, and Bancroft turned to him and asked his advice. He replied: "Do as you will, sir. I am of the chief's opinion. The red race has been cruelly outraged and robbed. But as a white man I know that the Indian must disappear. If you are an honest man and go to-day, to-morrow another will come to carry on your work. I warn you, however, that the chief is in earnest."

He, too, rose, as if to put an end to further questioning. I went up to him and said: "Sir, will you let me go with you? I promise to do or say nothing that will annoy you. It is only because I feel extraordinary interest in Intschu-Tschuna, and even more in Winnetou."

That he himself was included in this interest I dared not say.

"Yes, come with me a little way," he replied. "I have withdrawn from my race, and must know them no more; but since you have crossed my path, there can be no harm in our meeting, and some good may result from it. We will walk a little together. You seem to me the most intelligent of these men; am I right?"

"I am the youngest, and not clever, and I should be honored if you allowed me to go with you," I answered respectfully.

"Come, then," said Kleki-Petrah kindly, and we walked slowly away from the camp.

CHAPTER VI.

A WISH AND ITS TRAGIC FULFILMENT.

"You do not speak like a Westerner," said Kleki-Petrah as we started.

"No, I am from the East," I replied. "I came here to see the world."

"A bad thing to see sometimes. I am a German. It must seem strange to you to find a German become a full-fledged Apache."

"God's ways seem marvellous, but they are natural after all."

"God's ways! Why do you say *God*, instead of destiny, fate, or fortune?"

"Because I am a Catholic, and recognize that the hand of God is in the affairs of men."

"You are right, and are happier than you know; never lose that conviction. Yes, it is true that God's ways often seem marvellous, but are perfectly natural. The greatest marvels are the fulfilment of His laws, and the daily actions of nature are the greatest marvels. A German, a student, a teacher of some renown, and now an Apache—these seem wonderful changes, but they came about naturally."

Though he had taken me with him half unwillingly, he seemed glad to speak of himself. We had not gone far from camp, and had lain down under a tree, where I could study his face and expression at leisure. The vicissitudes of life had engraved deep lines upon his brow; long furrows of sorrow, the marks of doubt and thought, the many seams of care and privation. Though his eyes might once have been piercing, angry, threatening, now they were as calm and clear as a forest lake.

I should not have dared to question him as to his evidently strange history, though I longed to know it, but he asked me all about myself, and my answers were so full and frank that they gave him evident pleasure.

When he had heard all there was to learn of me he bowed his head, saying: "You are at the beginning of the conflict which I am ending, but you need not fear. You have the good God with you who will never forsake you. It was otherwise with me. I had lost my God when I left home, or rather was driven from it, and instead of the staff of strong faith I took with me the worst companion a man can have—a bad conscience."

He looked at me as he said these words, and, seeing my face unchanged, asked: "Are you not shocked?"

"Nonsense! who could suspect you of a great crime? I doubt your being a thief or a murderer."

I laughed as I spoke, but he said gravely: "Thank you, but you are mistaken. I was a thief, for I stole much that was priceless. And I was a murderer, the worst of murderers, for I slew souls. I was a teacher in an advanced school, it does not matter where. I was born a Catholic, but lost my faith, and my greatest pride lay in being free and having dethroned God, and all my influence and skill went to robbing others of their faith. I had great power over men, and numberless were the hearers whom my lectures led into infidelity. Then came the revolution. He who acknowledges no God recognizes no king or authority as sacred. I placed myself at the head of a lawless band of malcontents, who acclaimed me as their leader, and we rose in mad rebellion against constituted authority. How many fell in that struggle! I was a murderer, and the murderer not only of these, but of others that perished later behind prison walls. I fled from my fatherland to escape a like fate. I had no father or mother, no brother or sister; not a soul wept for me, but many cursed me as the cause of their sorrow. In fleeing from the police I ran one day through a little garden and entered a dilapidated house, where I found an old mother and her daughter in direst need. They told me their pitiful story with bitter tears. They had been comfortable, the daughter married but a year to an honest man who earned enough for a decent livelihood. He had heard my lectures, and been led away by them. He persuaded his father-in-law to join him and take part in the rebellion under my leadership. The young man fell on what he thought a field of honor, but the old father was imprisoned. The women told me this not knowing it was their listener who was responsible for their wretchedness. God's mills began to grind. Freedom was mine still, but peace was gone. I wandered everywhere, but found no rest. I was often on the verge of suicide, but a hand held me back—God's hand. At last I reached the United States, and came to the West. In Kansas I met a priest, one of my own

A WISH AND ITS TRAGIC FULFILMENT. 63

countrymen, and he saved me. He dispelled my doubts, and gave me back faith and contentment. Dear Lord, I thank Thee for it."

He was silent awhile, with hands folded and gaze directed heavenward. Then he resumed: "I fled from the world and men to do penance, and turned towards the wilderness. I saw the red man's wrongs, and my heart overflowed with wrath and compassion. I resolved to atone as far as might be for my wrong to the white man by devotion to the red. I went among the Apaches, learned their tongue, and became their teacher. Winnetou is my especial charge; were he the son of a European lord he would be a renowned prince, for he is richly endowed by nature. Would that I might see him a Christian! But though I have taught him all I could of Catholic truth, it may never be, for he shrinks from deserting the religion of his ancestors. However it may end I will remain with him to the day of my death. He is my spiritual son; I love him more than myself, and it would be joy to me to receive in my own heart a shot intended for his, for I would gladly die for him, feeling that perhaps such a death might wash away the last stain of my sins."

His head sank on his breast, and I remained silent, feeling that anything I could say would be trivial after such a confession, but I took his hand and pressed it heartily. He understood, and returned the pressure.

After a time he spoke again. "Why have I told you this? I have seen you to-day for the first time, and probably we shall never meet again. Has it been by the inspiration of God? For I, the former blasphemer, now seek to find His will in all things. There is an indefinable feeling of melancholy in my heart, which is not exactly sorrow. It is like the feeling that comes to one when the autumn leaves are falling. How shall my tree of life shed its leaves? Gently and after they are sere, or shall it be cut down before its natural time has come?" He gazed in silence down the valley, where I saw Intschu-Tschuna and Winnetou returning. They were mounted now, and leading Kleki-Petrah's horse.

We rose to go to the camp, which we reached as the Indians came up. Rattler leaned against the wagon, his face on fire, for in the short time that had passed he had drunk as much as he possibly could, and was a horrible sight. His eyes were like a wild beast's, and I made up my mind to watch him, for he was dangerous.

The chief and Winnetou dismounted and came towards us. "Have my white brothers decided to go or stay?" asked Intschu-Tschuna.

The head engineer had thought of a compromise, and said: "We must stay here whether we would or not, and obey the command laid upon us. But we will send to Santa Fé and ask for instructions from those that sent us, and then we will answer."

This was a cunning thought, for by that time our work would be done. But the chief said decidedly: "I will not wait. My white brother must say at once what he will do."

Rattler had filled a glass with whisky, and came towards the two Indians, saying incoherently: "If the Indians will drink with me we will go, if not we won't.

A WISH AND ITS TRAGIC FULFILMENT.

Let the young one drink first. Here's fire-water, Winnetou."

He held out the glass. Winnetou stepped back in disgust.

"What! You won't drink with me? That's an insult. Here, take the whisky, you red dog; lick it up, if you won't drink it." Before any one could stop him, he had thrown the contents of the glass in the young Apache's face. According to Indian custom such an insult was to be avenged by death, but Winnetou merely struck him to the earth, while, like his father's, his face betrayed no sign of what he felt, and the drunkard picked himself up and staggered back to the wagon.

"Once more," said Intschu-Tschuna, "and this is the last time, I ask: Will the pale-faces leave our valley to-day?"

"We cannot," was the reply.

"Then remember there is strife between us."

I started towards them, but the three strangers turned back to their horses without noticing me.

From the wagon came Rattler's voice crying: "Get out, you red coyotes! but the young one shall pay for knocking me down." Quicker than it can be told he had snatched a gun from the wagon and aimed it at Winnetou, who was standing alone, without protection, where the bullet must have found him; nor was there time to warn him.

Kleki-Petrah cried in anguish: "Down, Winnetou, down," at the same time springing before the young Apache. The shot whistled through the air. Kleki-Petrah fell to the ground with one hand at his breast,

A WISH AND ITS TRAGIC FULFILMENT.

while at the same moment Rattler fell, struck by my hand. I had sprung at him as soon as I saw his intention, but too late.

A cry of horror arose from all sides; only the two Apaches were silent. They knelt by the friend who had given his life for them, and examined his wound. It was close to the heart, and the blood flowed from it in torrents. I, too, knelt by Kleki-Petrah, whose eyes were closed and whose face was fast growing white and drawn.

"Lay his head on your breast," I said to Winnetou. "If he sees you when he opens his eyes, his death will be happier."

Without a word Winnetou followed my suggestion, and his eyes never wandered from the dying man.

At last he opened his eyes, and seeing Winnetou bending over him a peaceful smile came over his suffering face, and he whispered: "Winnetou, O my son, Winnetou!" Then his failing eyes seemed to seek something, till he saw me, and he said to me in German: "Stay with him; be true to him; carry on my work."

He raised his hand imploringly; I took it, and replied: "I will, I promise you I will."

An ineffable expression came upon his face, and he murmured in a faint voice: "My leaves are cut off, not fading; it is—wiped out. I die—as—I—wished. God, forgive—forgive. Jesus, mercy—mercy—Mary, pray—mercy—" He folded his hands, a flood of blood burst from his wound, his head fell back: he was dead.

Now I knew what had led him to unburden his heart to me—the inspiration of God, as he had said. He had wished to die for Winnetou; how quickly had his wish

A WISH AND ITS TRAGIC FULFILMENT. 67

been fulfilled! The last trace of his sin had been washed away. God is love and infinite compassion; the contrite He will in no wise cast out.

Winnetou laid the dead man's head in the grass, slowly rose, and looked interrogatively at his father.

"There lies the murderer where I have struck him down; he is yours," I said.

"Fire-water!" Only this brief reply came from the chief's lips in contemptuous tones.

"I will be your friend, your brother; I will go with you." The words burst from me involuntarily.

Intschu-Tschuna spat in my face. "Miserable cur!" he said, "thief of our land, dare to follow us, and I will crush you!"

I let the insult pass, awed by the presence of the dead and my promise to him.

The white men stood dumbly waiting to see what the Apaches would do. They never glanced at us again. Placing the corpse on the horse which Kleki-Petrah had ridden, they bound it fast, took the bridle, and, mounting themselves, rode away.

They spoke no word, and as Sam Hawkins watched them disappear he said: "That is more dangerous than the most dreadful threats. We shall see trouble, and there lies the cause, with no mind or soul; what shall we do with him?"

I did not wait to hear the answer; I saddled my horse and rode away. I wished to be alone to escape hearing this last awful half-hour discussed. It was late in the evening when, weary and exhausted in body and soul, I returned to the camp.

CHAPTER VII.

A COMPACT WITH THE KIOWAS.

It was decided by our party that we were not able, under the circumstances, to punish Rattler for his crime, which was most unsatisfactory to my youthful sense of justice. Sam pointed out, however, that his punishment was swift and certain at the hands of the Apaches; but the drawback to this consolation was that we who were innocent were likely to suffer with the guilty. We knew that the Indians would return to avenge Kleki-Petrah's murder as soon as they could summon their warriors, and the most important thing for us was to discover where the main body of the braves were, how far the chief and his son must ride to come up with them, and consequently when we could expect their return. Bancroft was most anxious to finish our work before we left, provided there was time before the anticipated attack, and calculated that it would require five days to complete our task. So Sam Hawkins volunteered to ride on the trail of the chiefs who had visited us, to discover, if possible, all that we needed to know, and took me with him, partly for protection, because I had earned such a reputation for being able to strike a hard blow with what Sam called my "lily lady-fingers," partly that I might have experience in the art of following a trail,

A COMPACT WITH THE KIOWAS. 69

and partly, I hope, because he liked to have me with him.

I had not been able to eat or sleep the night after the murder, for I could not cease going over the dreadful scene. I saw myself seated by Kleki-Petrah, heard his story, which had become to me a dying confession, and thought again and again of his last words, expressing a presentiment of his coming death. Yes, the tree of his life had not fallen naturally, but had been violently cut down, and by what an assassin, for what a reason, and in what a manner! If there was any consolation to be found in the bloody work of that day, it was that Kleki-Petrah had died on Winnetou's heart, and he had received the shot intended for his beloved pupil.

But what of his request that I should cling to Winnetou and fulfil the work that he had begun? Only a few moments before he had said that we should probably never meet again, and indeed my path in life lay far enough from the Apaches, and yet he had left me a problem the solution of which would bring me into the most intimate relations with that tribe. Was this request but chance words? Or was the dying man in the last moment of his life, as his soul fluttered on the border of the next world, given a glimpse of the future? It seems so, for events enabled me to fulfil his wish, though then it appeared extremely unlikely that I should ever be brought into friendly contact with Winnetou.

But why above all had I so quickly given my pledge to the dying man? Through pity? Yes, undoubtedly; but there was another reason. Winnetou had made an impression upon me such as I had never received from any other man. He was exactly my age, yet of far greater parts, and this I felt from the first glance at him. The proud earnestness of his clear, velvety eyes, the quiet certainty of his bearing, and the profound sorrow on his fine young face had revealed it to me. How admirable had been his conduct and that of his father! And what a lesson for many a white man lay in Intschu-Tschuna's one word of explanation of Rattler's crime: "Fire-water!" These thoughts, and the dread of meeting as enemies, returned to slay me and my comrades, these two whom I not only liked, but whom I had promised to befriend, kept all sleep from my eyelids, and it was with a heavy heart that I set out with Sam on the following morning to ride on their trail.

We started early, before the sun had risen. It was my very first scouting expedition, and, though I have since taken many such rides, I can never forget this first one. The trail was easily followed, a fact which made Sam doubt its being trustworthy; for he said that when an Indian left his course so easily traced by an enemy the chance was it was done only to lead that enemy into a trap. But I felt sure that in this case it was only because the chief and Winnetou were too heavily encumbered by the corpse of Kleki-Petrah, and in too great haste to avenge his murder, to obliterate the trace of their course, and rode on with no fear of an ambush.

It was an hour before mid-day when we came to a thicket of young oaks where the Indians had evidently halted to cut saplings for a litter or drag for the body of Kleki-Petrah, for we saw the leaves and twigs which they had stripped from the young trees in its construction lying on the ground. Here Sam reined up, saying: "Now we've gone far enough; we'll rest awhile. Winnetou rode all night to this point; do you see that the trail goes on from here in single file? That means that they rode this way to cover the fact that one has gone on alone, for greater speed, leaving the other to follow with the body. The one in advance is probably the chief, and Winnetou has taken charge of his murdered teacher. This will enable Intschu-Tschuna to summon his braves quickly, and we may expect their return very soon, perhaps before the five days are up which you need for your work."

We let our horses, or rather my horse and Nancy, drink at a stream which flowed between the saplings, and we lay down to rest for half an hour before we turned to go back. We lay silent, I thinking of the approaching struggle with the Apaches, while I saw by the regular heaving of his breast that Sam slept. If I needed a proof of the intelligence of animals, and the keenness attained by the senses of both man and beast in a life in the wilds, I was to receive it now. The mule was tethered in the bushes, where she could see nothing, nibbling the leaves and grass; she was not a sociable beast and preferred to be alone, while my horse grazed close to my elbow. Suddenly Nancy uttered a short, sharp, I might almost say warning, note, and in an instant Sam was awake and on his feet.

"I was asleep, but Nancy woke me. Some man or beast is coming. Where is my mule?" he cried.

"Here in the bushes; this way."

We crawled through the undergrowth, and saw only

Nancy looking out through the branches. Her long ears waved excitedly, and her tail swung from side to side; but when she saw us coming she quieted down; ears and tail were still.

We peered out, and saw six Indians coming on the trail single file. The first one, a short but muscular man, kept his head down, apparently never raising his eyes from the trail. They all wore leather leggings and dark woollen shirts, and were armed with muskets, knives, and tomahawks. Their faces shone with grease, and across each one ran a red and a blue stripe.

"What a lucky meeting! They are Kiowas, and they'll save us," said Sam. "The one ahead is Bao, which means *Fox*, a daring and crafty warrior, as his name indicates. The chief of the band is called Tangua, a bold Indian, and a good friend of mine. They have their war-paint on, and apparently they also are reconnoitring."

The six warriors drew near while I was wondering how they could save us. Six Indians would not be much help, but it was a comfort to find that Sam knew them, and that at least we had nothing to fear from them. Sam stepped forth from the bushes, put his hands to his mouth, and uttered a peculiar sharp cry which they seemed to recognize, for they reined in their horses and shouted back. Again Sam called to them and signalled, and they understood both cry and signal, for, returning them, they galloped toward us.

"Is our white brother Sam here?" asked the leader as he came up. "How comes he in the path of his red friend and brother?"

"Bao, the crafty fox, has met me because he came upon my tracks," answered Sam.

"We thought they were the tracks of the red dogs we seek," said the Fox in broken but perfectly comprehensible English.

"What does my brother mean?"

"The Apaches of the tribe of Mascaleros."

"Why do you call them dogs? is there enmity between them and the brave Kiowas?"

"There is war between us and these scurvy coyotes."

"I am glad to hear it. My brothers may sit down with us, for I have something important to tell them."

The Fox looked at me searchingly, and said: "I have never seen this young pale-face; is he one of the warriors of the white men? Has he won a name?"

If Sam had told him my own name it would have made no impression, so he fell back on the name Wheeler had given me. "This is my dearest friend and brother, and though he is young he is a great warrior among his own people in the rising sun. Never in his life had he seen a buffalo, yet two days ago he fought with two bulls to save my life, and killed them, and yesterday he stabbed a grizzly bear of the Rockies with his knife, and received no scratch himself."

"Ugh! ugh!" grunted the Indians, regarding me approvingly.

"His bullet never misses its mark, and in his hand dwells such strength that at a blow from him his enemy falls to the ground. Therefore the white men of the West call him Old Shatterhand."

Thus without any choice of mine I was given the name which has ever since clung to me.

The Fox offered me his hand, and said in friendly tones: "If Old Shatterhand will, we will be friends and brothers. We love men who can knock down an enemy with a blow, and he shall be welcome among us."

Which really meant: "We need allies with such strength, so come to us."

However, I replied: "I love the red men, for they are the sons of the Great Spirit, whose children we also are. We are brothers, and will unite against all enemies who do not respect us."

A smirk of satisfaction passed over his greased and painted face as he replied: "Old Shatterhand has spoken well; we will smoke the pipe of peace with him." So saying he seated himself, and brought out a pipe which he filled with a mixture apparently of red turnip, hemp, chopped acorns, and sour sorrel, lighted it, rose, took a whiff, puffed it towards heaven and earth, and said: "Above dwells the Great Spirit, and here on earth exist the plants and beasts which he made for the Kiowa warriors." Then he took another whiff, and blew it towards the north, east, south, and west, saying: "In all directions dwell the red and white men who wrongfully take these beasts and plants for themselves; but we shall find them, and take what is ours. I have spoken. How!"

What a speech! This Kiowa openly declared his tribe the owner of everything, and hence robbery was not only his right but his duty. And I must treat this sort of people as friends!

The Fox handed the pipe to Sam, who took half a dozen puffs and said: "The Great Spirit judges not the appearance of men, nor can they deceive Him by painting their faces, for He sees the heart. The hearts of the warriors of the glorious tribe of the Kiowas are brave and wise. Mine is bound to them as my mule is tied to the tree, and will be so forever. I have spoken. How!"

That was just like Sam, the artful, jolly little man, who always knew how to win his hearers, and yet have his joke.

And now it was my turn to take the foul pipe and become eloquent. I also rose, took a whiff, and—yes, the turnip, hemp, acorns, sour sorrel were all there in the pipe-bowl, but there seemed to be a fifth ingredient in the mixture, for it tasted as if it had bits of felt shoes in it. I puffed the smoke towards the earth and the sky and said: "The sunshine and air come from Heaven, whence come all good gifts. The earth receives the warmth and moisture, and gives them to the buffalo and mustang and bear and deer, to the pumpkin and corn and all good plants from which the red man makes his kinnikinnic, that in the pipe of peace breathes brotherly love."

I had read that Indians call their tobacco "kinnikinnic," and the knowledge opportunely came back to me now. A second time I filled my mouth with smoke and blew it toward heaven, and continued: "In the west rise the Rocky Mountains, and to the east stretch the plains; on the north roll the seas, and the south is washed by the waters of the great ocean. Were all the land between these points mine I would share it with the warriors of the Kiowas, for they are my brothers. This year may they kill ten times as many buffaloes and fifty times as many grizzly bears as they number. May their corn grow as large as pumpkins, and their pumpkins so great that twenty could be made from one. I have spoken. How!"

These wishes were not very practical, but they seemed to please the Indians as much as if they were already fulfilled. The Fox seized my hand, assured me of his friendship for all time, then took the pipe between his teeth, and smoked in supreme content.

Having brought the Indians into a state of high good humor, Sam said: "My brothers say that the war-hatchet has been dug up between them and the Apaches of the Mascaleros. How long has this been so? and what has ended the peace between them?"

"Since the time two weeks ago, when the Apache dogs killed four of our warriors."

"Where?"

"At Rio Pecos."

"That is not your camp, but that of the Mascaleros; what were your warriors doing there?"

The Kiowa did not hesitate to reply candidly: "A band of our braves went at night to capture some of the Apaches' horses. The vile dogs watch well; they killed our brave men. Therefore we have taken up the war-hatchet."

So the Kiowas had intended to steal, yet would make the Apaches atone for their defence of their own property. I would have expressed my mind on this conduct, but Sam signalled to me so energetically to be quiet that I obeyed him, and he said: "My brother the Fox is out to spy; when will his braves follow?"

"They are one day behind us."

"Who leads them?"

"Tangua, the chief himself, at the head of two hundred braves."

"And you expect to overcome the Apaches?"

"We will come upon them as the eagle swoops on the heron that has not seen him."

"My brother is mistaken. The Apaches know that they are to be attacked by the Kiowas."

The Fox shook his head incredulously, and replied: "How could they know it? Do their ears reach to the tent of the Kiowas?"

"Yes."

"I do not understand my brother Sam; he must tell me what he means."

"The Apaches have ears which can walk and ride; yesterday we saw two such ears that had been listening at the camp of the Kiowas."

"Uff! Two ears. Two scouts?"

"Yes. My brothers have not considered everything. Intschu-Tschuna, the chief of the Apaches, is a very wise warrior. When he saw that his people had killed four Kiowas he said to himself that the Kiowas would be avenged, and set out to spy upon·you."

"Uff! uff! He himself?"

"Yes, and his son Winnetou."

"Uff! He too? Had we known that, we would have captured the two dogs. I must hasten back to tell this to the chief, that he may call out more braves. We are enough for a surprise, but not if we are expected. Will Sam and Old Shatterhand ride with me?"

"Yes; not to Tangua, the chief of the Kiowas, but to our camp."

"That I cannot do."

"Hear what I say. Would you take Intschu-Tschuna, the chief of the Apaches, a prisoner alive?"

"Uff!" cried the Kiowa as if electrified, and his voice was ear-splitting. Then he said: "If my brother has a jest on his tongue I will not bear it."

"Nonsense! I am in earnest. In five or six days at most, and I can't tell how much sooner, you can capture the chief and his son Winnetou alive."

"Where?"

"In our camp; and you'll see how if you listen to what I tell you."

Sam then told the Indian of our road, to which they had no objection, and of our meeting with the Apaches. As he ended he said: "I wondered to see the two chiefs alone, and decided they were buffalo-hunting and had parted from their followers for a little time, but now I see it all. They were out reconnoitring, and the fact that the two heads of the tribe made this ride themselves shows they considered it an important matter. Now they will thirst for a double vengeance: on you, and on us for Kleki-Petrah's murder. They will send a smaller band against us than against you, and the chief and his son will be with the former. After we have shown you our camp, that you may find it again, you will go back to your chief, tell him all I have said, and he will come with his two hundred braves to wait for Intschu-

Tschuna with his little band. We are twenty strong, and of course will help you, and it will be child's play to capture the Apaches. It is like having the whole tribe to have the chiefs, for you can demand of them what you will. Does my brother see it all?"

"Yes; my white brother's plan is very good, and we will start at once to reach his camp before dark."

We mounted and galloped towards the camp, cutting across by a shorter route, since it was no longer necessary to follow the trail. I was shocked at Sam Hawkins and very angry with him. Winnetou, the noble Winnetou, and his father were to be betrayed into a trap, which if successful would destroy them! How could Hawkins have formed such a scheme? I tried in vain to get him apart from the Kiowas to ask an explanation; but he seemed to suspect my intention, and stuck close to the Fox, which made me angrier than ever.

When we got into camp I sprang from my horse, and lay down on the grass in no very happy frame of mind. Disregarding all my signals to him, Sam had taken the Indians to our men, who were in a high state of delight when they learned they had come in friendship and there was no longer any reason for our fearing the Apaches.

After the Kiowas had been hospitably received and entertained, Sam came to me for the first time. "You have a long face to-night," he said. "Is it real indigestion or mental colic? I suspect it's the latter; open your heart to me and I'll cure you."

"I'd be glad if you could, Sam, but I doubt it."

"Yes, I can; only try me."

"Tell me, then, how Winnetou struck you?"

"As a fine fellow, just as he did you."

"Yet you will betray him to his death; how does that hang together?"

"To his death! I? That's impossible for my father's son."

"But you'll make him a prisoner of these villains, and that means death."

"Don't believe that fairy tale. On the contrary, I'd do a good deal to save Winnetou if he were in danger."

"Then why do you set this trap? And listen, Sam. If he is captured, I'll free him; and if a weapon is turned on him, I'll stand by his side and fight for him. I warn you of this frankly. I promised a dying man to be his friend, and that is as binding to me as an oath."

"I like that, I like that," Sam announced. "We agree there."

"Oh, yes," I exclaimed impatiently, "you say so, but how do your good words agree with your actions?"

"So that is what you want to know, hey? Old Sam Hawkins suspected you wanted to speak to him, but he dared not let you. He's a different fellow than he seems, only he's not going to show his cards to any one but you and Dick Stone and Will Parker, who are to help in his plot. We were lucky to have met the Kiowas and learned all we know now, and I really don't see any other way of saving ourselves from the Apaches. However much you may admire Winnetou, you'd have to love him in eternity, for, being ignorant of your devotion to him, he'd send you there in short order. Now the Kiowas will come here with their two hundred braves— "

" I'll warn Winnetou," I interrupted.

" Heaven forbid ! " cried Sam. " That would only ruin us, for the Apaches would put an end to us and the Kiowas together. No, they must actually be face to face with death; and if then we secretly free them, as we will, they'll be grateful, and forego all revenge on us. At most they'll only demand Rattler of us, and I would not object to that. What do you say now, my angry gentleman ? "

I gave him my hand, and replied: " I am perfectly satisfied, my dear Sam; you've thought it all out well."

" Haven't I ? Hawkins has his good side, after all. Are we friends again ? "

" Yes, old Sam, and I'm sorry I was so suspicious."

" Then put your head down and sleep, for to-morrow there's a good deal to do. I'll go now and look up Stone and Parker, to let them know where we stand. Good night, and trust me better next time."

Wasn't he a kind, trusty fellow, this queer old Sam Hawkins ?

CHAPTER VIII.

SAM HAWKINS GOES SPYING.

WHEN Sam left me I tried to sleep, but it was long before I succeeded. The camp was noisy over the coming of the Kiowas and our rescue thereby, and besides my own thoughts were not soothing. Hawkins had spoken of his plans confidently, as though they could not miscarry; but after I was left alone I was not so sure of them. We were to free Winnetou and his father, but nothing had been said of the other Apaches. Would they remain in the hands of the Kiowas when their chiefs were rescued ? We four men could scarcely liberate all the Apaches, especially as it was to be done so secretly that no suspicion could fall on us. And how were the Apaches to come into the hands of the Kiowas ? Hardly without a struggle, and it was easy to foresee that these very two whom we wished to deliver would defend themselves most bravely, and hence be in the greatest danger of death. How could we prevent this ? I thought long over these problems, twisting myself into every imaginable position, but could find no way out of the difficulty. The only thought which comforted me in a measure was that clever, trusty little Sam would find a way out; and as to myself, I determined to stand by the chiefs, and if necessary defend them with my life. So at last I went to sleep.

The next morning I went at my work with redoubled energy to make up for the previous day's absence. Each man did his best, so we went forward far more rapidly than usual, and by night had doubled the amount of work done the day before, of course moving the camp onward as we worked. We were equally industrious on the next day till noon, when an interruption came in the shape of the Kiowas.

These Indians arrived just as the sun was highest; they were of strong fighting build, all armed with guns, tomahawks, and knives. Their leader was of truly imposing size, with a sharp, sinister face, and a pair of knavish eyes that spoke no good of their owner. When I saw his face I thought it would go hard with Intschu-Tschuna and Winnetou if they fell into his hands. He was called Tangua, a word meaning *Chief*. Though he was there as our friend and ally, he treated us in a manner far from friendly, but came like a tiger that had joined a leopard after prey and would rend his ally the next moment.

As the chief came up he did not dismount to greet us, but made a comprehensive salute with his hand, including us all, and rode straight to our wagon and lifted the cover to look in. Its contents seemed to please him, for he dismounted and got into the wagon to examine them.

"Oho!" cried Sam Hawkins, standing beside me, "he appears to want to make up his mind as to our property before he says a word. If he thinks Sam Hawkins is stupid enough to stand like a hitching-post, he makes a mistake, as I'll show him pretty quick."

"No rashness, Sam," I begged. "These two hundred fellows are too much for us."

"In numbers, yes; in wit, no," he answered. "It looks as though we had taken pretty poor accomplices, but come over to the wagon and hearken how Sam Hawkins talks to such rascals. I'm well acquainted with this Tangua, and if he doesn't know I'm here he'll have to find it out. Come on."

We had our guns in our hands, and proceeded to the wagon where Tangua was rummaging. Sam asked in a warning tone: "Does the glorious chief of the Kiowas wish to go instantly to the Happy Hunting Grounds?"

The Indian, whose back was toward us, stooping over, straightened himself, turned to us, and answered gruffly: "Why does the pale-face interrupt me with this silly question? Tangua will rule as a great chief in the Happy Hunting Grounds in the end, but a long time must pass before he journeys there."

"That time may come in one minute."

"Why?"

"Get out of the wagon and I'll tell you; only be quick about it."

"I will stay here."

"Good; then go up in a burst," said Sam, turning as if to go away.

The chief sprang from the wagon, seized Sam's arm, and cried: "Go up in a burst! Why does Sam Hawkins speak such words?"

"To warn you of death, which would have grabbed you in a moment if you stayed there."

"Uff! Is death in that wagon? Show him to me!"

"Later, maybe. Have not your spies told you why we are here?"

"I learned from them that you wish to make a road for the fire-horse of the pale-faces."

"That's it, and such a road goes over rivers, under ground, and through rocks; you know that, and you may have heard of the stuff with which we blow up the mighty rocks which are in the way of our fire-horse's feet. Is it that powder with which we load our guns?"

"No; the pale-faces have made another discovery by which they can overthrow whole mountains."

"Right; and this discovery we carry in that wagon, done up in packages, and if you touch it carelessly it will explode in your hands and blow you into a thousand pieces."

"Uff! uff!" he grunted, evidently shocked. "Was I near one of these packages?"

"So near that if you had not sprung down you would be this moment in the Happy Hunting Grounds. And what would you have had with you? No medicine, no scalp-lock, nothing, nothing at all, but little bits of flesh and bones. How could you rule as a great chief in the Happy Hunting Grounds in such a state? You would have been crushed under foot by the spirit-horses. An Indian who comes to the Happy Hunting Grounds without medicine or scalp-locks will be received by the dead heroes with contempt, and have to hide from their eyes, while they drink deep of all Indian joys; this is the belief of the red man. What a misfortune, then, to arrive shattered into little bits!"

One could see under the dark skin that the shock had driven the blood from the chief's face, and he cried: "Ugh! how good that you warned me in time!"

"Because we are friends and brothers," said Sam.

"I will go and warn my braves, lest they go near that dangerous wagon and suffer death," said Tangua.

"Do so, I pray you; for not only they, but you and I and all here would be blown up with them. If one who does not understand how to use this discovery were to touch it he would blow up his friends as well as his enemies, while in our hands it is sure to blow up those whom we choose to dispose of. Let us warn your braves, and at the same time remind them that they have not yet greeted their white brothers."

With this happy hint of the possible consequences of offending us, and reminder of his omission, coupled with a sly wink at me, Sam accompanied the chief to his braves.

The Kiowas and our three scouts held a conference to discuss the best means for carrying out the capture of the Apaches, while we surveyors continued working until darkness forced us to discontinue.

We seated ourselves all together around the fire after supper, and the camp presented to me, unused to such a scene, a picture of the greatest interest. Sam Hawkins and his two inseparable companions sat near me; around the blazing fire were the redskins, their greased faces shining in its light, while just beyond the horses were grazing, and dimly seen in the distance were the sentinels which the chief had stationed there. As I looked from one copper-colored face to another I saw none which I would have trusted to show compassion to an enemy.

I asked Sam the result of the conference. "You may be satisfied," he said. "Nothing will happen to your two darlings."

"But if they should try to defend themselves?"

"It will never come to that; they will be overcome before they have a chance to know what has happened. We know which way they are coming; do you?"

"They'll go to the spot where they found us the other day, and follow on our trail."

"Right; you're not so stupid as you look. Then we're certain of the first thing we must know, and that is the direction from which we're to expect them. The next thing is to find out the time."

"That can't be known exactly, but I suppose you can guess it pretty closely."

"Yes, if a man has any brains he can guess well enough, but guessing won't do for us. Any one who acts on guesswork in such circumstances as these takes his skin to market. Certainty, absolute certainty is what we must have."

"We can only get that by sending out spies, and you put your veto on that; you said the track of spies would betray us."

"Indian spies; mark that—Indian spies. The Apaches know we are here, and if they came upon the footprint of a white man it would not make them suspicious. But if they found the footprint of an Indian it would be very different; they would be warned. And since you are so wise, can you guess what they would suspect?"

"That the Kiowas were here."

"Yes, you have actually guessed it. If I did not need my old wig myself I'd crown you with it; consider it done."

"Thanks, Sam; I'll try to deserve the honor. But now look here: you mean that we should send white spies after the Apaches; is that it?"

"Not *spies;* only one."

"Is that enough?"

"Yes, if that one's a fellow to be trusted, called Sam Hawkins. Do you know the man?"

"I know if he undertakes a thing we need feel no more anxiety. He won't let the Apaches catch him."

"No, not catch him, but see him. I mean to let them see me wandering around, so they'll think we feel as safe as in Abraham's bosom. They won't touch me, because if I didn't come back your suspicions would be aroused."

"Suppose they see you and you don't see them?" I hinted.

"I seen and not see!" he exclaimed in pretended wrath. "If you give me such a box on the ear as that it's all over between us. Sam Hawkins's eyes may be little, but they're sharp. As soon as I have seen them I'll slip back to you, that you may be warned when their spies are coming, and act perfectly at ease."

"But they'll see the Kiowas if they send spies here," I objected.

"Who will they see? Kiowas? Man, tenderfoot, most respected youngster, do you think Sam Hawkins's brains are made of cotton-wool or tissue-paper? Our dear friends the Kiowas will be safely hidden, so there won't be the smallest trace of them; see? Then when the Apache scouts have gone back to the braves, I'll crawl after them and see when the whole body moves. They'll come by night, and we'll burn our camp-fire so we can be plainly seen. As long as it lasts the Apaches will certainly stay hidden. We will let it burn out, and as soon as it is dark steal over to the Kiowas. Then the Apaches will come—and find no one! Of course they'll be astonished, and light up the fire again to look for us, when we shall see them as plainly as we were seen before, and we'll reverse the game and fall on them. Isn't that a stroke? It will be talked of long, and every one will say: 'Sam Hawkins planned that little business.'"

"Yes, it's very fine, if everything goes as you expect. And after that shall we free the Apaches?"

"Intschu-Tschuna and Winnetou at least, and any others we can."

"And what will happen to the rest?"

"Nothing bad, I'm sure. The Kiowas will be too busy at first looking for the chiefs. But it's time enough to plan the next step when we've got through this one. What comes later we'll take care of later. The next thing to do is to select a good spot for carrying out our scheme, and that I'll attend to the first thing in the morning. We've talked enough to-day; to-morrow we must act."

He was right; there was nothing else to do now but await events.

The night was not very comfortable; a high wind arose, increasing to a gale, and towards morning it grew unusually cold for that region. We were awakened chilled to our marrows. Sam scanned the sky, and then said: "Apparently we are going to have rain to-day, and that happens rarely about here, but is the very best thing for our plan."

"Why?" I asked.

"Don't you know why?" replied Sam. "Look around here and see how the grass is flattened down. The one thing I was afraid of was that when the Apaches came it would show them that there was a greater number of men and horses here than they saw. But if it rains it will wash away all trace of this, and the grass will spring up again as fresh as ever. I must set out to look for the place where we will let the Apaches overtake us, and the Kiowas must go with me before the rain comes, so it can wash away their tracks. In the meantime you can work in peace."

He went over to lay his plan before the Kiowas, and in a short time all the Indians rode away with Sam and his two companions. We followed them slowly step by step as our work advanced, and towards noon Sam's prophecy was fulfilled; it rained, and in such torrents as can only fall in those latitudes. It seemed as though an ocean were falling from the skies.

In the midst of this torrent Sam came back with

Dick and Will. We did not see him until he was within twelve or fifteen feet of us, so thick was the veil of rain before us. They had found a suitable place; Stone and Parker were to remain and show it to us. But in spite of the weather Hawkins went back, as soon as he had laid in provisions, to resume his office of spy. As he disappeared in the thick rain I felt that misfortune was close upon us, and a sense of loneliness and dread came over me like a pall.

CHAPTER IX.

WAITING THE ONSLAUGHT.

THE rain ceased as suddenly as it began, and the sun shone down on us as warm as on the day before. We worked rapidly till nightfall, and a few hours' labor in the morning brought us to a stream swollen by the late rain, flowing beside a small open savanna, which was bordered on one hand by trees and shrubs. A wooded peninsula ran out into the water, and beside the stream rose a gentle elevation crowned by thick woods.

"This is the place Sam picked out," said Stone, looking at it with an air of recognition. "There couldn't be a better place for our purpose. The Kiowas are so hidden you might try hard and not find the least trace of them, yet I know they see us perfectly. The savanna is covered with a growth that makes it easy for the Apache spies to conceal themselves and follow us unseen. Then look at the open plain of grass leading here. A camp-fire burning on it will light all the savanna, and hide the Apaches, so they can easily come upon us."

His lean, weather-beaten face gleamed with satisfaction, but the head engineer did not share the feeling. He shook his head, saying: "What is the matter with you? Do you mean to say you rejoice that we can be so easily overcome? I tell you it's far from pleasant to me; I am paralyzed at the mere thought."

"The surer to fall into the hands of the Apaches," cried Stone. "Don't let such feelings get hold of you, Mr. Bancroft. Of course I'm glad, for the easier the Apaches can overtake us, the easier we can capture them. Just look here. Over there on the heights are the Kiowas in the midst of the woods. Their spies sit in the highest trees, and have surely seen us coming, and in the same way they'll see the Apaches, for they can look all across the savanna."

"Well, what earthly good will it do us, if we're overtaken, to have the Kiowas look across the savanna?"

"Don't you see? They stay there only because here the Apaches would see them. As soon as their scouts have come and gone the Kiowas will come over to us, hide on the peninsula, and we'll put our horses at its neck, for then the Apaches will keep off it, as the horses would neigh if they went near them, and give us warning. The Apaches will hide, and wait till we're asleep—"

"Suppose they shouldn't wait?" I interrupted.

"That wouldn't be dangerous for us," he replied. "The Kiowas would come to our assistance at once."

"But then there'd be bloodshed, which we want to avoid."

"Yes, but here in the West a drop of blood doesn't count. Don't worry; the Apaches are sure to wait, for they know that if awake we'd defend ourselves, and though we'd get the worst of it, still some of them would be sure to get killed, and they value their blood as highly as we do ours. Therefore they'll wait till we lie down to sleep; then we'll let the fire go out, and go over to the island."

Now that we were on the scene of action, and the hour was so near, I was greatly perturbed in mind. I was not afraid, but I was anxious, apprehensive of the result, and worried as to the fate of Winnetou, of whom I had thought so much during the past few days that he had grown near and dear to me, although he was still my enemy; and it must have been a kind of mental telepathy, for I learned later that he had been thinking continuously of me. Since the encounter could not be avoided, I wished it might come soon and be over with; and this wish was to be fulfilled.

It was a little short of mid-day when we saw Sam Hawkins returning. The little man was weary, but his eyes gleamed with unusual fire.

" All's well ? " I asked. " But I see it is, dear old Sam."

" Do you ? " he laughed. " Where is it written, on my nose or in your imagination ? "

" No one who sees your eyes can doubt it."

" So my eyes betray me; that's good to know for another time. But you're right; everything is really better than I could have hoped."

" Have you seen the spies ? "

" Seen the spies! I've not only seen 'em, but I've seen the whole band; and not only seen 'em, but heard and watched 'em."

" Watched them ! Then tell us, quick, what you've discovered."

"Gather up your instruments, and go into camp while I go over to the Kiowas to tell them what their part is to be. I'll be back pretty soon."

He sprang across the stream, and disappeared into the woods, while we packed up our instruments, and went back to camp to await his coming. We neither saw nor heard him till he stood among us, saying: "Here I am, my lords; haven't you eyes and ears? Now that shows you how you can get close to men without their knowing it; and that's the way I did yesterday with the Apaches."

"Tell us; tell us."

"You shall hear; but I must sit down, for I'm pretty tired. My bones are used to riding, and don't enjoy walking any more; besides, it's grander to belong to the cavalry than to the infantry."

He sat down near me, and then said, nodding his head positively: "We'll have the ball to-night."

"To-night!" I echoed, half shocked, half glad. "That's good."

"H'm! you seem to be in a hurry to fall into the hands of the Apaches. However, you're right; it is good, and I'm glad, too, that we won't have to wait any longer. It's no fun waiting when you don't know how a thing will turn out."

"Don't know! Is there any reason for anxiety?"

"Not a bit; on the contrary, I'm certain everything will go well. But any man of experience knows that the best child may grow up bad, the finest plans take a wrong turn from some unforeseen cause."

"Well, do tell us what you heard. Hurry up."

"Softly, softly, my young sir; everything in order. I can't tell you what I heard, because you must first know how I heard it. When I went out in the rain from here I went back to where we were camping when the two Apaches came to us, and had to hide at once, for there were three redskins sniffing around. Apache spies, says I to myself; and so they were. They surveyed the premises without coming on my trail, and sat down under the trees where it was dry to wait for their chiefs, and I had to wait, too, two long hours. At last came a mounted band, led by Intschu-Tschuna and Winnetou."

"How many were there?"

"Just as I expected, about fifty men. The spies went out to meet them, and after a few words with their chiefs went on ahead, the braves following slowly. You may imagine, gentlemen, that Sam Hawkins followed after them. The rain had washed out ordinary tracks, but the broad trail of your camp was plain; I wish I might always have a trail as easy to follow. But the Indians wanted to be very sure, for they peered into every nook and corner and behind every bush, and made such slow progress that darkness came on after we had gone only about two miles, and they dismounted and made their camp."

"And did you creep up to them there?"

"Yes; like wise fellows they made no fire, but Sam Hawkins, being equally wise, thought that served him as well as them. So I crawled under the trees, and wriggled forward on my stomach till I got near enough to hear what they were saying. Their words were brief but to the point. It is as we expected: they want to capture us alive."

"And not kill us?"

"Not all at once. They want to take us to the Mascaleros village at Rio Pecos, where we are to be tortured and die a living death, like carp taken out of the water and put into a pond to fatten. I wonder what kind of flesh old Sam's would make, especially if they put me into the pan in my leather hunting-jacket."

He laughed in his silent, inward fashion, and added: "They've got their eye on Mr. Rattler there, sitting as still as if heaven, with all the saints, were waiting for him. Yes, Rattler, they've got a banquet ready for you that I wouldn't care to sit down to. You're to be spitted, impaled, poisoned, smothered, shot, broken on a wheel, and hanged, each done a little more beautifully than the other, and only a taste of each that you may be kept alive a long time and have the full benefit of all the torture and anguish of death. And if after all you shouldn't be quite dead, you're to be laid in the grave of Kleki-Petrah, whom you murdered, and buried alive."

"Merciful Heaven! did they say that?" gasped Rattler, his face blanched with terror.

"That's what they said, and you deserve it. I only hope if you do escape you'll be half decent in the future; and I guess you will be, for the body of Kleki-Petrah will be a strong medicine for you."

"Where is the main band of the Apaches which is out against the Kiowas?" I asked.

"I don't know; nothing was said of that. It doesn't matter to us."

Little Sam was mistaken in that; it was far from unimportant to us where this band was, as we discovered in a few days.

Sam continued: "As I had heard enough, I should have come back to you at once; but it was dark, and I couldn't see the trail till dawn, so I waited. I stayed all night hidden in the wood, and my legs were almost broken. I was six miles from here, and I had to go out of my way to get back unseen. And that is all I have to tell you."

"But you said you were going to show yourself to them."

"I know, and I should have done so, only—hark! did you hear anything?"

The scream of an eagle, thrice repeated, came from the woods.

"That's the Kiowa spies," he said. "They are over there in the trees. I told them to give me this sign when they saw the Apaches on the savanna. Come, sir; we'll try what sort of eyes you have."

This invitation was addressed to me. Sam rose to go, and I took my gun to follow him.

"Hold on," he said. "Leave that gun here. It's true the frontiersman should never go out without his weapons, but this is an exception, because we must not seem to have any suspicion of danger. We'll appear to be gathering wood to make our fire, and the Apaches will conclude we are going to stay here all night."

We sauntered out, apparently wandering carelessly in

and out among the trees and bushes, breaking off the dry branches. We strained our eyes, but could discover no one; yet later I learned from Winnetou himself that fifty feet at most away from us he was hidden behind a bush watching us. We gathered more wood for the camp-fire than we needed, for Sam wanted enough in reserve to enable the Apaches to kindle the fire quickly when they discovered we were gone.

Darkness fell, and we gathered in the camp for the eventful night. Sam, as the most experienced, sat at the end of the grassy plain nearest the savanna, where he could see the coming of the spies for whom we were waiting, knowing they could not be far off. The fire blazed up, lighting the plain and the savanna. How foolish and inexperienced the Apaches must think us! This great fire was the very thing to guide an enemy to us from afar. We ate our supper, and lounged about as if we were far from suspecting any danger. The guns lay at some distance back of us towards the peninsula, ready to be seized by us later in our flight.

Three hours after dark Sam stepped back to us and said softly: "The spies are coming; two, one on this, one on that side. I heard and saw them." Then he sat down with us, and began to talk in a loud voice on the first subject that occurred to him. We answered, and kept up a conversation intended to show the spies how secure we felt. We knew that they were there watching us, but by a strong effort we kept ourselves from glancing towards the bushes concealing them.

The most important thing now was to know when they had gone. We could neither hear nor see anything, and yet we dared not waste a moment after their departure, for in a short time the whole band would be upon us, and in that interval the Kiowas must come over from the peninsula. Hence it was best not to wait until they had withdrawn, but to force them out. So Sam rose as if he were going to get more wood, and went into the bushes on one side, while I took the other.

We were now sure that the spies were gone. Sam put one hand to his mouth and thrice imitated the croaking of a bull-frog. This was the signal for the Kiowas to come; it would not be noticed by the Apaches, as we were beside the stream. Sam then resumed his office of watchman to warn us of the approach of the whole body of the enemy.

About two minutes after the signal was given the Kiowas came over, in close single file—a long line of two hundred warriors. They had not waited in the woods, but had come down to the bank to be ready for the signal, and on receiving it had instantly sprung across the stream. They crawled behind us in our shadow like snakes, lying close to the ground, near the peninsula. This was done so quickly and silently that in three minutes, at the most, the last one had joined us. In a short time Sam came and whispered to us: "They're coming on both sides. Don't put on any more wood; we must let the fire die down, and take care that an ember is left for the Indians to kindle another."

We piled what wood we had left around the fire, so that no light would fall upon our retreat. After this was done each of us had to be more or less an actor. We knew that fifty Apaches were close to us, yet that we

WAITING THE ONSLAUGHT.

must not betray our knowledge by the slightest sign. We expected them to wait until we were asleep; but what if they did not wait, but fell upon us at once? Of course we had two hundred allies in the Kiowas, but in that case there would be a bloody struggle that might easily cost some of us our lives.

The time had come, and it was interesting to watch the various effects it produced on my comrades. Rattler lay face downward on the ground as if asleep, the fear of death gripping his heart with an icy hand. His trusty friends glanced at one another with blanched faces; they could not utter a word to help on our forced conversation. Will Parker and Dick Stone sat there as calmly as if there were no such thing as an Apache in the world. Sam Hawkins made jokes, and I laughed in spite of myself at his nonsense. For now that the danger was upon us I was as calm as if we were about to play a game of whist. And so we waited.

CHAPTER X.

THE CAPTURE OF WINNETOU.

For more than an hour we sat waiting the attack, and then concluded that we had been right and the Apaches would not come until we were asleep. The fire was getting low, and I thought there was no use in putting off the evil hour, so I yawned, stretched myself, and said: "I'm tired, and I'd like to go to sleep; how about you, Sam?"

"I've no objection," he said. "The fire is going out anyway. Good night, then."

"Good night," repeated all, and getting back from the fire as far as we could we stretched ourselves out at full length. The flame grew dimmer and dimmer, till it died out altogether, only the ashes still glowing; but the light could not reach us because of the wood piled between us and the fire, and we lay entirely in the shadow.

Now was the time to get quietly, very quietly, into safety. I reached for my gun, and slowly crept away. Sam kept at my side, the others following. When I reached the horses I stirred them up that the noise of their stamping might cover any possible rustling we might make in going. We came over safely to the Kiowas, who stood like panthers crouching for prey.

"Sam," I whispered, "if we want to spare the two

chiefs we mustn't let a Kiowa get at them: understand?"

"Yes."

"I'll take Winnetou; you and Stone and Parker look after Intschu-Tschuna."

"One for you alone, and one for us three together? That's no way to do."

"Yes, it is. I'll finish up Winnetou in short order, and there should be three to take charge of his father, for his braves will be around him, and if he should resist it would cost him his life."

"Well, all right. We'd better go on a few steps and be first, or some Kiowa will get ahead of us. Come."

We posted ourselves a little in advance, and awaited in greatest suspense the war-cry of the Apaches. It is customary for an Indian leader to give the signal for an onslaught by a cry in which the rest join like demons. This is intended to deprive the victim of all courage, and is well adapted to its end. The best idea one can get of it is by uttering a long-drawn-out $H\text{-}i\text{-}i\text{-}i\text{-}i\text{-}i\text{-}h$ at the top of his voice, at the same time striking the mouth repeatedly with the hand to break the sound into waves.

The Kiowas were at as high a tension as we were; each of them wanted to be first, and pushed us forward further and further till we were too near the Apaches for comfort, and I wished very heartily the onslaught might come.

At last it did come. The $H\text{-}i\text{-}i\text{-}i\text{-}i\text{-}i\text{-}h$ arose in such a tone as to go through my very marrow, followed by a howl as dreadful as if a thousand devils had broken loose. We heard quick steps and springs over the soft earth. Suddenly all was still; for a moment we could almost have heard an ant crawl. Then we heard Intschu-Tschuna speak the short word: "Ko." This means "fire," or "make a fire." The ashes of our fire were still smouldering, and as the Apaches obeyed him and threw the dry wood on them, it kindled at once, and the flames leaped up anew, lighting the entire camp.

Intschu-Tschuna and Winnetou stood side by side, and a circle of braves gathered around them as the Apaches saw to their amazement that we were gone. "Uff! uff!" they grunted in astonishment. Winnetou then showed that presence of mind which later so often excited my wonder. He saw that we could not be far off, and that they, standing in the full light of the fire, made a fine mark for our guns; therefore he cried: "Tatischa! tatischa!" which means: "Be off!"

He had turned to spring away, when I stood before him, and for a moment we looked each other in the face. Quick as lightning his hand was at his knife, but before he could draw it I struck him in the temple. He staggered and fell to the ground, and I saw that Sam, Will, and Dick had overpowered his father. The Apaches howled in rage, but their cry was hardly audible, for it was drowned by the horrible din of the Kiowas, who now sprang upon them. As I had broken through the Apache circle, I stood in the midst of a fighting, howling tangle of men, struggling together. There were two hundred Kiowas against fifty Apaches, four to one, yet these brave warriors defended themselves with all their strength. I had all I could do to protect myself, and had to take a hand in the fight, since I was in the midst of it; but I used my fists only, as I had no desire to harm any one. After I had knocked down four or five, and had space to breathe in, I saw the struggle was becoming feebler, and five minutes after it began the whole thing was over.

Only five minutes; but under such circumstances five minutes seem a long time. Intschu-Tschuna lay on the ground, and Winnetou beside him, both bound. Not an Apache had escaped, for none of the brave fellows had once thought of deserting his chief and making off through the darkness. Many of them were wounded, as were some of the Kiowas, of whom three were killed and five Apaches, which was exactly what we had hoped to avoid, but they had made such fierce resistance that the Kiowas had drawn their knives. The besieging party was all bound, and now came the question of disposing of the prisoners. I wanted to make it as easy for them as possible, but Tangua, the Kiowa chief, said imperatively: "These dogs are ours, not yours, and I will decide what is to be done with them. I would take them to our village, but we don't want to be long on the way, for their people might overtake us, and we have far to go. We will put them to death by torture here."

"I think you make a mistake," I remarked.

"How?"

"In saying they belong to you. That is false."

"It is true."

"No; by the laws of the West a prisoner belongs to his captor. Take the Apaches you captured, but those we captured belong to us."

"Uff! uff! how wise you speak! So you want to keep Intschu-Tschuna and Winnetou. But what if I won't allow it?"

"You will allow it."

He spoke angrily, but I answered him gently, though firmly. He drew his knife, thrust it into the earth up to the handle, and said with flashing eyes: "If you lay a hand on a single Apache your body shall be like this earth in which my knife stands. I have spoken. How!"

This was said in deadly earnest; but I would have shown him that I was not afraid of him if Sam Hawkins had not given me a warning glance which kept me silent.

The captive Apaches lay around the fire, and it would have been easier to leave them there where they could be watched with no trouble, but Tangua wanted to show me they were really his property to do with as he pleased, and ordered them tied to the trees near by. This was done, and none too tenderly, the two chiefs being treated most roughly, and their fetters drawn so tight as to make the blood burst from the swollen flesh. It was absolutely impossible for a prisoner to break away and escape unaided, and Tangua set guards around the camp to prevent rescue.

Our second fire burned in the same place as the first one, and we sat around it alone, the Kiowas being as anxious to stay by themselves as we were to have them do so. They had not shown themselves friendly towards us from the first, and my late encounter with their chief was not calculated to make them more so. The looks of hatred which they cast upon us did not invite to confidence, and we felt that we might be glad if we escaped with no further clash with them. They considered themselves the lords of the situation, and regarded us as the big lion in the menagerie regards the little dog he tolerates near him.

Sam, Dick, Will, and I were thinking about the execution of our plan to free the chiefs, which was made the more difficult in so far that only we could share in it. We dared not let our comrades into our secret, for they would certainly oppose it, if not betray it to the Kiowas.

We sat together a long time, how long I could not tell, for I had not yet learned to tell time by the position of the stars, but it must have been till a little past midnight. Our companions slept, our fire had burned low, and all the Kiowas' fires were out but one. Sam whispered to me: "All four of us cannot undertake this; two only are necessary."

"Of whom of course I'm one," I answered softly.

"Not so fast, dear boy; the matter is at the risk of life."

"I know that."

"And you want to risk your life?"

"Yes."

"Well, you're a brave fellow, but you'd not only risk your own, but the lives of the two captives."

"Of course."

"I'm glad you admit it, for then I think you'll leave it to me."

"Not much."

"Be reasonable. You know nothing about spying, and experience is necessary for such a job. It must be born in a man to do these things, and then he must know how to use his talent."

"I'll prove I'm fit for it. Look here: do you know whether Tangua is asleep or not?"

"No."

"And yet it is important, isn't it?"

"Yes; I'll crawl over and find out."

"No, but I will, and prove I'm fit for the other job."

"Suppose you're discovered?"

"Then I'll say I wanted to make sure the guards were doing their duty."

"That'll go, but for mercy's sake be careful. If they see you they'll suspect you later of freeing the Apaches if they get off."

"They won't be far wrong."

"Take each tree and shrub for a cover, and look out that the firelight doesn't fall on you; keep in the dark."

"I'll keep dark, Sam."

"I hope so; and if you succeed I'll give you credit for it, and think maybe after ten years you may amount to something."

I stuck my knife and revolver deep in my belt, not to lose them on the way, and crept away from the fire. Now as I tell it, I know the awful risk I took so lightly. I had no idea of spying on the chief; I wanted to set Intschu-Tschuna and Winnetou free. I had set my heart on doing it myself, but Sam Hawkins stood in the way of my desire with his caution. Even if I did succeed in spying on Tangua, I was afraid Sam would not let me go to Winnetou, so I thought I would better make sure of going while I had a chance. In doing this I not only risked my own life and the lives of the Indians, but those of my comrades; for if I were discovered it was all up with them, and I knew this quite well, but it made little impression on my youthful self-confidence. Nor did the fact that I had never crawled silently among enemies, Indian fashion, deter me in the least; I felt perfectly sure of success.

The distance between our fire and the spot where Intschu-Tschuna and Winnetou were bound was not more than fifty feet. I knew the best way to creep there was on the fingers and toes; but it needed strength in these members which I did not possess, so I crawled on my hands and knees like a quadruped. Before I put a hand down I first felt the spot to make sure there were no twigs that would crackle under the weight of my body and thus betray me; and if I had to go under or between branches I tested them carefully to make sure that I could get through. So of course I went slowly, very, very slowly, but I did make some progress.

The Apaches were tied to trees on each side of the grassy plain, the two chiefs on the left from our campfire. The trees stood at the edge of the grass, and scarcely five feet away sat the Indian, appointed especially to watch them because of their importance. This would make my task very difficult, perhaps impossible; but I had a plan for distracting his attention, at least for a moment, though to carry it out I needed stones, and none seemed to be within reach.

I had put perhaps half my way behind me, and had

been gone over half an hour—twenty-five feet in half an hour!—when I saw something gleaming at one side, and crawling over to it found to my great delight a small depression in the earth filled with sand that was washed into it by the recent rain and the overflow of the little stream. I filled my pocket with the sand and crept on.

After another good half-hour I found myself at last behind Winnetou and his father, possibly four feet away. The trees to which they were bound, with their backs towards me, were not broad enough to cover me, but luckily a leafy branch stood out at the foot of them which hid me from the guard. A few feet behind him, again, there was a thorny bush upon which I had designs.

I crawled first behind Winnetou, and there lay still a few minutes to observe the guard. He seemed tired, for his eyes drooped as if it cost him an effort to keep them open, for which I was grateful. Now I must find out how Winnetou was fastened. I reached cautiously around the trunk of the tree, and felt of his feet and legs. Of course he perceived this, and I feared he would make a movement which would betray me, but he was much too wise and had too much presence of mind for that. I found his feet were tied together and bound by a thong to the tree, so that two knife-cuts would be necessary. I saw by the flickering firelight that his hands were crossed from right to left and bound backward to the tree, and one cut would suffice to loose them. Now something occurred to me of which I had not thought before: when Winnetou was freed he might take to flight instantly, and that would put me in the greatest danger. I thought and thought, but could find no way out of the difficulty; I must risk it, and if the Apache sprang away at once I must save myself with equal speed.

How mistaken I was in Winnetou! I did not know him. We have discussed his liberation since, and he has told me that when he first felt my hand he believed it to be an Apache's. True, all whom he had brought with him were captured, but it was possible that he had been followed by a scout to bring him news of the main body of his braves. He was sure that he was to be freed, and waited confidently the cutting of his bonds. But he certainly would not fly at once, for he would not go without his father, nor would he endanger the life of him who freed him.

I cut the two lower bands; the upper ones I could not reach in my present position without risk of cutting Winnetou's hands. So I must stand up, and it was nearly certain the guard would see me. But I had brought the sand for such a moment. I thrust my hand into my pocket, took out a handful of it, and threw it past the guard into the bush behind him. This made a rustle; the Indian turned and looked at the bush. A second handful aroused his attention thoroughly—a poisonous reptile might be hidden in there—and he rose, turned around, and examined it carefully. Quick as a flash I had cut the thongs. In doing so I felt Winnetou's splendid hair in my eyes, and I seized a strand in my left hand, cut it off with the right, and then sank to the ground again. Why did I do this? To have proof that it was really I who had freed him.

To my delight Winnetou did not make the slightest motion, but stood precisely as before. I wound the hair into a ring and put it in my pocket. Then I crawled behind Intschu-Tschuna, whose fastenings I examined as I had Winnetou's, and found him bound exactly as his son had been, and he remained equally unmoved when he felt my hand. Again I cut the lower thongs first; then I succeeded in distracting the guard's attention as before, and freed the chief's hands. He was as considerate as his son, and made no movement. It occurred to me that it would be better not to let the thongs lie on the ground, for if the Kiowas found them cut they might suspect us. So I took Intschu-Tschuna's bands away, crept back to Winnetou and got his, and then began my journey back.

I had to make what haste I could, for when the chiefs disappeared an alarm would at once be given, and I dared not be anywhere around. I crawled farther into the bushes to be out of sight if this happened, and made my way back faster than I had come, but still cautiously. When I got close to the camp I lay flat, and made the rest of the way by wriggling along. My three comrades were alarmed about me, and as I again lay down between them Sam whispered: "We were worried about you. Do you know how long you've been? Almost two hours."

"I shouldn't wonder; half an hour going and half an hour coming, and an hour there."

"Why on earth did you stay so long?"

THE CAPTURE OF WINNETOU.

"To be sure the chief was asleep."

"Good gracious! Dick and Will, hear this tenderfoot! To make sure the chief was asleep, he stared at him a whole hour!"

"Never mind; I proved to you I could crawl."

I was keeping my eyes strained on the two Apaches, wondering why they delayed going. The reason was very simple: each was uncertain that the other had been freed, and they stayed for a signal from their liberator. As this was not forthcoming, Winnetou waited till he saw the guard's eyelids droop, when he motioned with his hand to his father, and the chief returned the signal; then they disappeared from their places.

"Yes, you have given us proof," said Sam Hawkins, answering my last remark; "but if you think you could free the two chiefs by piercing their bonds with your eyes for one full, precious hour, you're mistaken. It's a difficult thing anyway; I'm not sure it can be done, but if it can—good heavens! what is that?"

That instant the Apaches had vanished. I pretended not to see, and asked: "What's up? Why don't you go on?"

"Because—am I blind or not?"

He rubbed his eyes, and cried: "Yes, by thunder! it's so. Look yonder; are Intschu-Tschuna and Winnetou there?"

Before any one could answer the guard sprang up, stared a moment at the deserted trees, and then uttered a piercing cry that awakened every sleeper. The guard announced in his own vernacular what had happened, and a tumult began which was beyond description.

Every one ran to the trees, white men and red, I following. But on my way I turned my pocket wrong side out and got rid of the rest of the sand.

More than two hundred men surrounded the spot on which but a moment before the two chiefs had stood. A howl of rage arose which told me plainly what would be my fate if the truth came to light.

Tangua ordered half his men to disperse over the savanna, and search for the missing men as well as they could in the darkness. He actually foamed with rage. He struck the negligent guard in the face, tore his medicine-charm from his neck and trod it under foot. This was an everlasting disgrace, for the medicine-charm means everything to an Indian, and to lose it is to lose honor, and be an outcast from his tribe until he shall rehabilitate himself by killing an enemy and seizing his charm, which will then be considered as the victor's own. The guard took his bitter punishment without a word, shouldered his gun, and disappeared among the trees.

The chief's rage was directed not only against this unfortunate Indian, but against me. He strode up to me, and shrieked: "You wanted to keep those two dogs for yourself; go after them and catch them."

I was turning from him without answering, but he caught me by the arm, saying: "Did you hear my command? Obey."

I shook him off, and replied: "You cannot order me to obey you."

"Yes, for I am the chief of all this camp."

I drew from my pocket the tin box in which I kept

my papers, and said: "Shall I give you your proper answer, and blow up all your people? Speak another word to displease me, and I'll destroy you all with this medicine that blows up the mountains."

I was doubtful that this absurd statement would be believed, but it was. He drew back, crying: "Uff! uff! Keep your medicine for yourself, and be a dog like the Apaches."

We white men went back to our fire, and naturally the topic of conversation was the escape and how it came about. I did not reveal the secret even to Sam, Dick, or Will. I was very happy in its possession, and at the success of my attempt, which every moment of the vain search for the fugitives made more certain.

The lock of Winnetou's hair I have kept through all my wanderings in the West, and I have it safe to-day, a reminder not only of a mad adventure, but of a true friend.

CHAPTER XI.

A DIFFERENCE OF OPINION.

THE Kiowas' manner was such as to convince us that we would do well to look after our own safety, and we dared not lie down to rest without leaving one of our party on guard. We spent the night sleeping by turns, and early in the morning our sentinel awakened us to say that the Kiowas were following the trail of the fugitives, for which they had been obliged to wait till dawn. We in turn followed them, and the trail led us to the spot where Intschu-Tschuna and Winnetou had left their horses, and where they had mounted and ridden away. We surveyors resumed our work; we dared not lose a moment, for the Indians were sure to return to rescue their comrades and execute their twofold revenge, and we could not know how soon this might be, for we had no idea where the main body of the Apaches lay.

We worked hard till noon, when Sam Hawkins came to me and said: "There seems to be something up among the Kiowas in regard to the prisoners."

"Something? Don't you know what?"

"They seem to be getting ready to kill them, and to do it soon, for they are preparing the torture now."

"We must stop that."

"Now look here; the Kiowas are two hundred strong.

Do you mean to say you can stop their doing what they please?"

"I hope not to be obliged to do it alone; I count on you and Dick and Will, and I have full confidence you won't forsake me, but will do your utmost to prevent such wholesale murder."

"So you have confidence in us! I'm very grateful for it, for it's no trifle to have the confidence of such a man as you."

"Listen, Sam; I'm in earnest. The fate of so many men is not a subject for jesting."

He gave me a whimsical glance out of his little eyes. "The dickens! So you're in earnest! Then I must pull a long face. But do you consider the situation? We are only four against two hundred, for we can't count on the others. Do you think we could possibly succeed, or do you mean to live up to your new name of Old Shatterhand, and knock down all the two hundred warriors with your fist?"

"Nonsense! I didn't give myself that name, and I know well enough we can't do anything against two hundred; but must it come to force? Cunning is often better."

"Now I wonder if you read that in your books? You'll become prudent if you don't look out, and I'd like to see how you'd seem in that shape. I tell you there's nothing to be done here with all your cunning. The Indians will do what they please, and not care a rap whether you like it or lump it."

"All right; I see I can't depend on you, and I'll have to act alone."

"For mercy's sake, don't do anything foolish. You won't have to act alone, for, whatever you do, we'll stand by you. But it's not been my habit to run my head against thick walls, for I know the walls are harder than the head."

"And I never said I'd do the impossible. But if there's any way to save the Apaches, we must find it."

"Certainly; but what way is there?"

"I've been thinking I'd force the chief to do my will by holding a knife to his breast."

"And stab him?"

"If he wouldn't give in, yes."

"Good powers above! you're mad," he cried, shocked.

"I assure you I'll try it."

"It's—it's—" Sam checked himself, his surprised and anxious face taking on another expression, until at last he said: "I don't know as it's such a bad idea, after all. Nothing but force would make Tangua yield, and with a knife at his breast he might— Well, actually, a greenhorn can have a small, so-called idea once in a while."

"The first thing is to get the chief away from his braves. Where is he now?"

"Over there with them."

"Will you get him off, Sam? Tell him I want to speak to him and can't leave my work."

"I doubt if that'll work; however, I'll try. Suppose he brings some of his men with him?"

"I'll leave them to you and Stone and Parker; I'll take care of Tangua. Have thongs ready to bind him; the thing must be done quietly and quickly."

"Well, I don't know how the plan's going to work, but, as nothing else occurs to me, you shall have your way. We risk our lives, and I have no desire to die, but I think we may come out of it with a black eye."

He laughed in his usual quiet manner, and went off.

My companions were too far away to have heard what we had been saying, and it never occurred to me to tell them our plan, for I was sure they would have prevented its execution. They valued their own lives more than those of the captive Apaches, and I realized what a risk I ran. But I felt I ought to give Stone and Parker a chance to withdraw if they chose, and asked them if they wanted to take a hand in the game. Stone replied: "What is the matter with you? Do you think we're sneaks to leave a friend in the lurch? Your scheme is a stroke worthy of a true frontiersman, and we'll be glad to take a hand; isn't that so, Will?"

"Yes," said Parker. "I'd like to see if we four ain't the fellows to beat two hundred Indians."

I went on measuring, and did not look back until Stone cried: "Get ready; they're coming."

I looked, and saw Sam approaching with Tangua and three other Indians.

"A man for each," I said. "I'll take the chief. Throttle them so they can't scream, and wait till I grab Tangua; don't move first."

We went over towards the Indians, and took up our position where a bush screened us from the rest of the Kiowas left to guard the prisoners. The chief's face was none too friendly, and he said in equally unfriendly tone as he came up: "The pale-face called Old Shatterhand has asked me to come. Have you forgotten I am chief of the Kiowas, and you should have come to me, not I to you?"

"I know you are the chief," I answered.

"I have come because you have been a short time among us, and have yet to learn politeness. Speak briefly, for I have no time."

"What have you to do that is so important?"

"We are going to make the Apache dogs howl."

"Why so soon? I thought you were going to take them to your village, and torture them in the presence of your women and children."

"We wanted to, but they would hinder us on the war-path, whither we now go; so we shall kill them to-day."

"I ask you not to do this."

"It is not for you to ask."

"Can't you speak as civilly as I do to you? I only said I *asked* you; if I had commanded you, you might have had an excuse for being rude."

"I want to hear nothing from you, and a command is out of the question. No pale-face shall meddle in my affairs."

"Have you a right to kill the prisoners? No, don't answer, for I know what you will say; but there is a difference between putting men to death quickly and painlessly, and slowly torturing them. We shall never allow that where we are."

He drew himself up to his full height, and said scornfully: "Whom do you think I am? Compared with me you are like a toad which would attack a bear of the Rockies. The prisoners are mine, and I shall do what I please with them."

"They fell into your hands by our help, so we have the same right to them that you have, and we wish them to live."

"Wish what you please, you white cur; I laugh at your words."

He spat at me, and would have turned away, but I let drive and knocked him down. He had a hard skull, however, and, not being quite unconscious, tried to rise. So I had to give him another blow before I could pay any attention to the others. I saw Sam Hawkins kneeling on an Indian whom he had seized by the throat; Stone and Parker held the second one down, while the third ran shrieking away. I came to Sam's assistance, and we bound our man as Dick and Will finished up theirs. "That was foolish of you; why did you let the third escape?" I said.

"Because Stone and I went for the same one. We lost only two seconds by it, but it was enough to let that rascal escape."

"No matter," said Sam. "It only means that the ball will begin earlier. In two or three minutes the Indians will be upon us, and we must take care to have a free field between us."

The surveyors had seen our action with horror, and the head engineer came bounding over to us, crying: "What is the matter with you people? What have you done? We shall all be killed."

"You certainly will if you don't join us now," said Sam. "Call your people over here, and come with us; we'll protect you."

"Protect us—" Bancroft began, but Sam interrupted him.

"Silence!" the little man said sternly. "We know what we're about. If you don't stick to us you're lost. Come on."

We carried the three Indians to the open prairie, where we halted and laid them down, for we knew an open plain where we could see all around was safer than a position that afforded hiding-places. Scarcely had we got there than we heard the Kiowas' howls of rage, and after a moment they came running towards us; but as one ran faster than another they were strung out in a long line, not coming in a solid body; which was lucky for us, as in the latter case it would have been harder to bring them to a stand.

Plucky little Sam went a short distance towards them, and threw up both arms as a signal to stop. I heard him call out something which I did not understand. It had no effect until it was repeated, then I saw the first Kiowa, as well as the one next to him, pause. Sam spoke to them, pointing at us. Then I called upon Stone and Parker to raise the chief, and swung a knife over his breast. The Indians howled indignantly. Sam spoke further to them, and then one of them, next to Tangua in authority, came out from the rest and proceeded towards us. As they came up Sam pointed at our three prisoners and said: "You see I spoke the truth. They are entirely in our power."

The under-chief, whose face betrayed the fury within him, replied: " I see that these two Indians are alive, but the chief seems to be dead."

" He is not dead. Old Shatterhand's fist knocked him down, and he is unconscious, but he will soon revive. Sit down and wait; when the chief comes to himself again we will treat with you. But the moment one of the Kiowas touches a weapon Old Shatterhand's knife will be plunged into Tangua's heart."

" How dare you raise your hand against us who are your friends ? "

" Friends ! You don't believe that yourself when you say it."

" I do believe it; have we not smoked the pipe of peace together ? "

" Yes, but we can't trust this peace. Is it customary for friends to insult one another ? "

" No."

" Yet your chief insulted Old Shatterhand. See, he begins to move."

Tangua, whom Stone and Parker had laid down again, raised himself, looking at us at first as though he did not feel sure what had happened, then he recovered consciousness perfectly and cried: " Take off these bands."

" Why did you not listen to my request ? " I asked. " You can't give orders here." He gave me a look of rage, and snarled:

" Silence, boy, or I'll tear your eyes out."

" Silence is more fit for you than for me," I answered. " You insulted me, and I knocked you down. Old Shatterhand does not let go unpunished him who calls him a toad and a white dog."

"I will be free in a moment. If you do not obey me, my warriors shall wipe you from off the earth."

"You'd go first. Hear what I have to say. There stand your people; if one of them moves a foot without permission, my knife goes into your heart. How!"

I set the knife-point against his breast. He saw that he was in our power, and could not doubt that I would fulfil my threat. There was a pause, during which he seemed to long to annihilate us with his wildly rolling eyes; then he tried to control his rage, and asked more mildly:

"What do you want of me?"

"Nothing except what I have already told you: that the Apaches shall not die by torture."

"Then you ask that they shall not die?"

"Do with them later what you will, but while we are with you nothing must happen to them."

Again he considered a while in silence. Through the war-paint on his face we saw pass over it varying expressions of anger, hatred, and malice. I expected that the contest of words between us would be long, so wondered not a little when he said: "It shall be as you wish; yes, I will do more than that if you will fulfil the condition I will make."

"What is the condition?"

"First I want to tell you that you need not think I fear your knife. If you stabbed me, you would be torn to shreds in a moment by my warriors. No matter how strong you are, you cannot fight two hundred foes. So

I laugh at your threat to stab me. If I told you I would not do as you wish, you could do nothing to me. Nevertheless the Apache dogs shall not be tortured; I will even promise not to kill them if you will fight in a life-and-death combat for them."

"With whom?"

"With one of my warriors, whom I will choose."

"What weapons?"

"Only knives. If he kills you, the Apaches must also die; but if you kill him, they shall live."

"And be free?"

"Yes."

I could not help seeing that he considered me the most dangerous of his white allies, and wanted to get rid of me; for it goes without saying that his champion would be skilled in the use of the knife. Nevertheless, after short consideration I answered: "I agree; we will smoke the pipe of covenant, then the combat may begin."

"What are you talking about?" cried Sam. "You can't be so foolish as to go into such a fight."

"It is not folly, my dear Sam."

"The greatest folly possible. In a fair fight the chances would be equal, but they're far from so here. Did you ever have a fight to the death with knives?"

"No."

"There; you see? Your opponent will, of course, be skilled with the knife. And then think of the consequences of such a fight. If you die, the Apaches die, too; but if you kill your adversary, who is the worse for it? No one."

"But if I win, the Apaches get their lives and freedom."

"Do you really believe that?"

"Certainly; for it will be sealed by the solemn pipe of covenant."

"The devil's truth will be in such an oath, which covers some double meaning. And even if it is meant honestly, you are a tenderfoot and—"

"Now give us a rest with your 'tenderfoot,' Sam," I interrupted. "You've been shown that this tenderfoot knows what he is about."

Although Dick Stone and Will Parker joined Sam in imploring me to give up the bargain, I persisted, and at last Sam cried impatiently: "No good, boys; he must go on running his thick head against stone walls; I'll say no more against it. But I'll see it's a fair fight, and woe to him who cheats you! I'll blow him into a thousand pieces with my Liddy, and they'll be lost in the clouds."

The arrangements for the combat were now made. Two circles were drawn in the sand, touching each other and forming a figure 8. Each contestant was to stand in one of these circles, and not step beyond it during the combat. There was to be no quarter; one must die, and his friends would not take revenge on his conqueror.

When everything was ready the bonds were removed from the chief, and we smoked the pipe that sealed his promise to me. The two other prisoners were freed, and the four Indians went off to fetch their champion and summon the braves to see the combat.

The surveyors all protested with me, but I paid no

attention to their words, and Sam said: "You are a marvellously rash fellow. You will be killed, and what shall I do in my old age? I must have a tenderfoot to abuse; whom shall I scold if you are gone?"

"Some other tenderfoot."

"That's easier said than done, for I'll never have another out-and-out hopeless greenhorn such as you are in all my life. Let me take your place. It's no matter if an old fellow dies, but a young—"

"Now hold your kind tongue, my dear old Sam," I interrupted. "It's better a hopeless greenhorn should die than a valuable, experienced scout. But I hope I shan't die."

"Well, I'd rather take your place; but if I can't, promise me to remember it's for life or death. Don't come any of your humane nonsense; remember, you're not dealing with a knight or a square man, but a rascal and a murderer, who will kill you if he can. So get ahead of him; don't hesitate. I'm afraid you'll be weakly scrupulous."

"I assure you I have no such idea. It's he or I, and I'll do my best that it shan't be I. There shall not be an ounce of relenting, I promise you. I'll save the lives of all the Apaches, and my own, at the price of his, if I can. It's life or death, as you say, my dear Sam, and I mean to live; don't fret. Say a prayer for me, if you remember how, and I know you do; and I think God will bless a fight for such a good cause. Hush; here they come."

CHAPTER XII.

A DUEL, AND CAPTURE BY THE APACHES.

THE Indians came slowly towards us; not all, but a large number of them, for Tangua had left a portion of them to guard the Apaches. On reaching the spot a hollow square was formed, of which three sides were filled in by Kiowas, our men occupying the fourth side.

The chief then gave a signal, and from the ranks of the Indians strode a warrior whose proportions were absolutely gigantic. Laying aside all his weapons except his knife, he stripped off his clothing to his waist. No one could look upon his knotted muscles and not be anxious for me. The chief led him into the middle of the square, and announced to us in a voice ringing with the certainty of triumph: "Here stands Metan-Akva [*Lightning Knife*], the strongest warrior of the Kiowas, whose knife no man has withstood; his enemy dies beneath his blows as though struck by lightning. He will fight Old Shatterhand, the pale-face."

"Lord help us!" whispered Sam to me; "he's a real Goliath. My dear boy, it's all up with you."

"Nonsense!"

"Don't forget there's only one way to conquer this fellow, and that is to make the fight a short one. Let the end be quick, for he can tire you out, and then you're lost. How's your pulse?"

A DUEL, AND CAPTURE BY THE APACHES. 129

He put his fingers on my wrist, counted, and then said: "Thank God, not more than sixty beats, and perfectly regular. You're not excited? Aren't you a bit afraid?"

"It wouldn't do to be upset or afraid in a case that depends on calm blood and eye. The chief has selected this giant because he is invincible, and we'll see whether he really is so or not."

While I was talking I, too, had stripped the upper part of my body, for, although it was not necessary, I did not wish it to appear that I desired to shield myself from the knife. I gave my gun and revolver to Sam, and stepped forth into the middle of the square. One could almost see the throbbing of good Sam Hawkins' heart, but I felt undisturbed, and confidence is the first requisite for a combat.

The chief summoned us to take our places. Lightning Knife looked me over contemptuously, and said in a loud voice: "The body of this feeble pale-face throbs with fear; is he afraid to enter the ring?"

Scarcely had these words been uttered than I stepped into the southward circle, thus bringing my back towards the sun, while it shone into my adversary's eyes and blinded him. This may seem like taking an unfair advantage, but considering I had never fought with knives before, while he was renowned for his skill with them, this did not make up for the advantages on his side, and it was perfectly fair. Tenderness towards my opponent was worse than foolish; any weakness on my part would not only have cost me my life, but the lives of the Apaches for whom I fought; so, though a life-

and-death combat is a horrible thing, I was forced to do my best to kill this Hercules.

"He is actually going to try," laughed Lightning Knife scornfully. "My knife shall drink his blood. The Great Spirit gives him into my hand by taking away his senses."

Among Indians this sort of preliminary fight with tongues is customary, and I should have been considered cowardly if I had stood silent, so I answered: "You fight with the mouth, but I have here a knife; take your place if you are not afraid."

He bounded into the other circle, crying angrily: "Afraid! Metan-Akva afraid! Did you hear that, ye Kiowa braves? I will have this white dog's life with my first stroke."

"My first stroke will be the end of you. Now silence. You should not be called Metan-Akva, but Avat-Ya [*Big Mouth*]."

"Avat-Ya, Avat-Ya! This coyote pig dares insult me; my blade shall eat his bowels."

This last threat was very short-sighted on his part, for it gave me a hint as to the manner and place in which his weapon would be used. So he did not mean to stab my heart, but give a knife-thrust below, and rip my body.

We stood quite close, so that neither had to bend much to reach his foe. Metan-Akva's right arm hung straight down; he held the knife so that the hilt rested on his little finger, and the blade stuck out from between the thumb and index-finger, the edge turned upward. This showed that I was right: he intended to strike upward from below, for if he were going to strike downward he would have held the knife in the opposite way, that is, so that the hilt lay against the thumb, with the blade thrust outward through the fist by the little finger. Then I knew the way in which I was to be attacked; now the main thing was to know the exact moment, which his eyes would tell me. I knew the peculiar flash of the eyes which in such cases precedes a blow.

I dropped my eyelids to let him feel more secure, but only watched him closer through the lashes. "Strike, dog!" he cried.

"Be silent, and act, you red thief!" I replied.

That was a great insult, which must be followed either by an angry answer or the attack, and the latter thereupon ensued.

An angry dilation of his pupil warned me, and the next moment his right arm struck quickly and forcibly upward to rip my body like an old coat. Had I been looking for a blow downward it would have been all over with me, but I parried his thrust with my knife, and cut him deeply in the forearm.

"Dog! swine!" he shrieked, dropping his knife in rage and pain.

"Don't talk; fight," I said, raising my arm, and then my knife was in his heart up to the hilt. I instantly drew it out. The stroke was so true that a little stream of red blood spurted out on me. My foe swung backward and forward, groaned, and fell to the earth dead.

A wrathful howl burst from the Indians, but only the chief moved; he came out from the others and knelt by my adversary, examined the wound, rose, and gave me a look which I shall not soon forget. It was eloquent of fear, hatred, amazement, and admiration. He would have gone away without a word, but I said: " Do you see that I am still in my place, while Metan-Akva has left his ? Who has conquered ? "

"You have," he answered angrily, and went away; but after taking five or six steps he turned back, and snarled at me: "You are a white son of the wicked spirit. Our medicine-men will find out your charm, and then you shall give up your life to us."

" Do what you like with your medicine-men, but keep your word with us."

" What word ? " he asked haughtily.

" That the Apaches should not be killed."

" We will not kill them; I have said it, and will hold to it."

" And they shall be free ? "

" Yes, they shall be free. What Tangua, the chief of the Kiowas, has said shall be done."

" Then I will go with my friends and untie them."

" I will do that myself when the time comes."

" It has come, for I have conquered."

" Silence ! Did we speak of the time ? "

" It was not specified, but it is evident—"

" Silence ! " he thundered again. " I will decide the time. We will not kill the Apache dogs, but can we help it if they die for want of food or drink ? How can I help it if they starve before I free them ? "

" Rascal ! " I cried.

" Dog, speak another word like that, and—"

He did not finish his threat, but checked himself,

looking me in the face, which could not have been pleasant to look upon.

I completed his interrupted sentence. "And I'll knock you down with my fist, you vilest of all liars."

He sprang back, drew his knife, growling: "You will not get near me again with your fist. If you come one step towards me I'll stab you."

"So your Lightning Knife said, and tried to do, but you see he lies there. I will consult my white friends as to what shall be done with the Apaches. But if you harm a hair of their heads, you are lost. Remember, I can blow you all up."

With these words I went back to Sam, who could not hear the conversation between the chief and me, because of the howling of the Indians. He sprang to meet me, seized both my hands, crying: "Welcome, my dear, dear boy! you have come back out of the jaws of death. Dick, Will, see here; what do you think of this tenderfoot? But foolhardy men are always the luckiest, and the worst root grows the biggest potato. When you went into that circle my heart stood still; I could not breathe, and my thoughts were full of how I'd carry out this tenderfoot's last will and testament. But a thrust, a stab, and the redskin rolled on the ground. Now we've gained our end, and the Apaches are free."

"You're mistaken there," I said.

"Mistaken? How so?"

"The chief made a mental reservation in his promise, which now comes to light."

"I mistrusted that," cried Sam. "What is his reservation?"

I repeated Tangua's words to him, and he was so angry that he instantly started off to see the chief. I resumed the clothing and weapons I had laid down, and thought over the situation. Evidently the Kiowas had been confident that Lightning Knife would kill me, and they were furious over the result of our encounter. They could not fall upon us, since it was a life-and-death fight, and the survivor was promised security; but they would find some excuse for a quarrel; of that we might be sure.

The chief was occupied attending to the body of the dead warrior, and Sam found him in no mood to lend an ear to his protests. He strode back to me in high dudgeon, and said: "The fellow absolutely refuses to keep his word. He means to starve the prisoners to death, and he calls that not killing them. But we'll keep our eyes open, and get a shot at him."

"Provided we don't get a shot that is a boomerang," I remarked.

"I think myself we'd better be ready to protect ourselves, for our life may be in danger any moment. Lord help us, the moment's come!" he cried. "The Apaches have arrived, and there'll be a lovely row. Get ready for the fight, gentlemen."

Over beyond, where the prisoners and their guards were, rose that instant the shrill *H-i-i-i-i-h*, the war-cry of the Apaches. Contrary to all expectation, Intschu-Tschuna and Winnetou had already come back with their warriors, and had attacked the camp of the Kiowas. Those who were near us paused in amazement,

A DUEL, AND CAPTURE BY THE APACHES. 135

and then the chief shouted: "The foe among our brothers! Quick, quick, and help them."

He would have rushed back, but Sam Hawkins cried: "You can't go; don't you see we are surrounded? Do you suppose the Apache chiefs are such fools as only to attack your guards and not know where you are?"

He spoke rapidly; but before he had quite finished, the awful, soul-piercing cry arose around us. We were standing, as already said, on an open prairie, and had been so occupied that the Apaches had crawled behind the bush which had served us in our attack on Tangua, and had surrounded us without our knowledge, and now sprang upon us from all sides in overpowering numbers. The Kiowas shot at them with some effect, but not enough to reckon.

"Don't kill an Apache; not one!" I shouted to our three scouts, for already the deadly battle raged around us.

The head engineer and the three surveyors defended themselves, and were cut down. While my eyes were riveted on this awful sight I did not see anything that went on around me. We were attacked by a considerable band, and separated from one another. Although we cried out to the Apaches that we were their friends, it had no effect: they flew at us with tomahawks, and we perforce had to defend ourselves, however loath to do so. With our guns wielded as clubs we struck down so many that we won a little breathing-time for ourselves, during which I looked about me. Sam, Parker, and Stone ran towards the bushes where the fight was still hot, and, after making sure that the surveyors were beyond help, I followed. I had scarcely reached the bush when Intschu-Tschuna himself came up. He and Winnetou had been with that band of Apaches which had captured the camp and freed their kinsmen. This achieved, both chiefs had run to the assistance of the main body which we had encountered, Intschu-Tschuna considerably in advance of his son.

As he bounded around the bush he saw me, and exclaiming: "Land-thief!" raised his silver-studded rifle to knock me down. I cried out to him that I was not his enemy, but he would not listen, only redoubling his efforts to strike me. There was but one thing to do: if I would not be overcome, perhaps killed, I must disable him. As he raised his arm again for a blow I threw away my gun, with which I had parried his strokes, hung on his neck by my left arm, and with my right fist gave him a blow on the temple. His rifle dropped, he staggered and fell. Then behind me a joyful voice cried: "That is Intschu-Tschuna, the chief of the Apache dogs. I must have his scalp."

Turning around I saw Tangua, the Kiowa chief, who had come upon the scene just as all this happened. He dropped his gun, drew his knife, and stooped over the unconscious Apache to scalp him. I seized his arm and said: "Take your hands off. I have conquered him; he is mine."

"Be silent, white vermin!" he snarled. "What have I to do with you? The chief is mine. Get out, or—" He finished his sentence by striking at me with his knife and seizing me with his left hand. I did not want to stab him, so did not draw my own knife, but threw myself upon him and tried to free myself from his grasp. Failing in this, I choked him till he could not move, and then bent over Intschu-Tschuna, whose face was bleeding from my knuckles. Just then I heard a rustle behind me, and turned to see whence it came. This movement saved me, for I received on the shoulder a violent blow which had been intended for my head, and would certainly have broken it. It came from Winnetou. He had been behind his father, as I have said before, and coming around the bush he saw me kneeling over the chief, who lay bleeding and apparently lifeless, and he promptly gave me the almost fatal blow with the butt of his gun. Then he dropped the gun, drew his knife, and fell upon me.

My position was as bad as it could be. The blow had shaken my whole body and lamed my arm. I tried to explain to Winnetou, but he gave me no chance for a word. He stabbed me, and the point of the knife struck the edge of the tin box in which I carried my papers, glanced up through my neck, and pierced my tongue, but for which it would certainly have entered my heart. Then Winnetou withdrew the knife, and held it ready for the second stroke, his hand at my throat. The fear of death doubled my strength; I could use only one arm and hand, and he lay across me sidewise. I caught his right hand, and squeezed it till he dropped the knife; then I seized his left arm at the elbow and pulled him over till he had to let go of my throat. Then I lifted his knees, and with all my strength pushed myself from under him, which threw the upper part of his body on the ground. The next moment I was on his back, and our positions were reversed.

The question now was how to hold him down, for if he got up I was lost. Setting one knee on his thigh and one on his arm, I caught him around the neck with my one useful arm, while with the other hand he was feeling for his knife, fortunately in vain. Now followed an awful struggle between us; yet could I have spoken, one word would have sufficed to clear up the situation, but blood flowed in streams from my mouth, and when I tried to speak with my pierced tongue I could only stammer unintelligibly.

Winnetou exerted all his strength to throw me off, but I lay on him like a mountain not to be gotten rid of. He began to gasp, and I pressed my fingers into his windpipe so tight that he could not breathe. Must I kill him? Not in any case. I freed his throat for a moment, and he instantly raised his head, which gave me the chance I wanted. One, two, three good blows with my fist in quick succession, and Winnetou was unconscious: I had conquered Winnetou the unconquered. I drew a deep, deep breath as well as I could and not draw down my throat the blood which filled my mouth and streamed as fast from the external wound. As I tried to rise I heard an angry howl from an Indian behind me, and received a blow on the head which knocked me senseless.

When I came to myself it was evening; so long had I lain unconscious. Everything seemed to me like a dream; I felt as though I had fallen down beside the wall of a mill-wheel, which could not turn because I was wedged between its paddles and the wall. The water rushed over me, and the force which should have turned the wheel pressed on me stronger and stronger till I thought that I should be crushed. All my limbs were in pain, especially my head and one shoulder. By degrees I realized that the mill was not a reality, but delirium, and the roaring and rushing was not water, but the result of the blow which had felled me. And the pain in my shoulder was not caused by a mill-wheel crushing me, but by the blow which Winnetou had given me. The blood flowed from my mouth; it rushed into my throat and choked me, and I awoke fully to myself.

"He moves; oh, thank God, he moves!" I heard Sam say. I had opened my eyes, but what I saw was far from consoling. We were still on the spot where the fight had taken place. Over twenty camp-fires were burning, between which certainly five hundred Apaches were moving about. Many were wounded, and a large number lay dead on two sides, the nearest being the Apaches, and those on the opposite side, a little farther away, the Kiowas. Around us were the captive Kiowas, all strongly bound; not one had escaped, and Tangua, the chief, was among them. At a little distance apart I saw a man lying with his body drawn together in a ring, for the evident purpose of being tortured. It was Rattler. His comrades were no longer alive, having been shot at once; but he, as the murderer of Kleki-Petrah, was reserved for a slow and agonizing death. I was bound hand and foot, as were Parker and Stone, who lay on my left. At my right I saw Sam

Hawkins, who was fastened by his feet, and his right hand was bound against his back, but his left hand was free, as I learned later, in order to tend me.

"Thank Heaven, you are conscious again, my dear Jack," he said, stroking my face lovingly with his free hand. "How do you feel? Do you want anything?" I tried to answer, but could not. I saw Sam bending over me with anxious eyes, but I heard and saw no more, for again I sank into unconsciousness.

Upon regaining my senses I felt myself in motion, and heard the tread of many horses' feet. I opened my eyes. I was lying on the skin of the grizzly bear I had killed, which was drawn together into a hammock and hung between two horses, which were thus bearing me somewhere. I lay so deep in the skin that I could see only the heads of the horses and the sky above me. The sun shone down on me, burning like molten lead, and swelling my veins. My mouth was swollen and full of blood; I tried to move my tongue, but could not. "Water, water," I tried to say, for I was consumed with thirst, but I could only utter a hoarse groan. I said to myself that it was all over with me, and tried to think of God, and make a true act of contrition, and ask the mercy I was so soon to need, and turn my eyes to the land on the shore of which I stood; but again weakness overcame me. This time I fought with Indians, buffaloes, and bears, rode for life and death over scorching plains, swam for months over shoreless seas—in short, had a fever, caused by my wounds, in which I struggled hard and long with death. Occasionally I heard Sam Hawkins' voice, but far, far away; occasionally, too, I saw a pair of dark, velvety eyes—Winnetou's eyes. Then I died, was laid in my coffin and buried. I heard the earth shovelled on the coffin, and lay in the ground a whole unbroken eternity, unable to move, till the lid of my coffin noiselessly slid off and disappeared. Was all this true ? Could I be dead ? I raised my hand to my forehead, and— "Hallelujah ! Oh, thank God ! He comes back from death; he is alive !" cried Sam.

CHAPTER XIII.

NURSED TO HEALTH FOR A CRUEL FATE.

As I opened my eyes again upon this world I saw Sam Hawkins bending over me, his face radiant with joy, and a little behind him were Dick Stone and Will Parker, tears of happiness in their honest eyes.

Sam took both my hands in his, pushed away the forest of beard where his mouth should be, and said: "Do you know how long you have lain here?" I answered only with a shake of the head. "Three weeks; three whole weeks. You have had a frightful fever, and became rigid—to all appearance dead. The Apaches would have buried you, but I could not believe you were gone, and begged so hard that Winnetou spoke to his father, who allowed you to remain unburied until decomposition should set in. I have to thank Winnetou for that; I must call him."

I closed my eyes, and lay still; no longer in the grave, but in a blessed languor, in weary content, only wishing to lie so forever and ever. I heard a step; a hand felt me over and moved my arm. Then I heard Winnetou's voice saying: "Is not Sam Hawkins mistaken? Has Selki-Lata [*Old Shatterhand*] really revived?"

"Yes, yes; we all three saw it. He answered my questions by movements of his head."

"It is marvellous, but it were better he had not come back, for he has returned to life but to be killed."

"But he is the Apaches' best friend," cried Sam.

"And yet he knocked me down twice."

"Because he had to. The first time he did it to save your life, for you would have defended yourself, and the Kiowas would have killed you. And the second time he had to defend himself from you. We tried to explain, but your braves would not hear us."

"Hawkins says this only to save himself."

"No, it is the truth."

"Your tongue lieth. Everything you have said to escape torture convinces us that you were even a greater enemy to us than the Kiowa dogs. You spied upon us and betrayed us. Had you been our friend you would have warned us of the Kiowas' coming. Your excuses any child could see through. Do you think Intschu-Tschuna and Winnetou are more stupid than children?"

"I think nothing of the sort. Old Shatterhand is unconscious again, or he could tell you that I have spoken the truth."

"Yes, he would lie as you do. The pale-faces are all liars and traitors. I have known but one white man in whom truth dwelt, and that was Kleki-Petrah, whom you murdered. I was almost deceived in Old Shatterhand. I observed his daring and his bodily strength, and wondered at it. Uprightness seemed seated in his eyes, and I thought I could love him. But he was a land-thief, like the rest; he did not prevent you from entrapping us, and twice he knocked me in the head with his fist. Why does the Great Spirit make such a man, and give him so false a heart?"

I wanted to look at him as he spoke, but my muscles would not obey my will. Yet as I heard these last words my eyelids lifted, and I saw him standing before me clad in a light linen garment and unarmed.

"He has opened his eyes again," cried Sam, and Winnetou bent over me, looking long and steadily into my eyes.

At last he said: "Can you speak?" I shook my head.

"Have you any pain?" I made the same reply.

"Be honest with me! When a man comes back from death he surely must speak the truth. Did you four men really want to free us?"

I nodded twice.

He waved his hand contemptuously, and cried excitedly: "Lies, lies, lies! Even on the brink of the grave, he lies! Had you told the truth I might have thought that at least you could improve, and ask my father to spare you. But you're not worth such intercession, and must die. We will nurse you carefully, that you may be sound and strong to bear long torture. A weak or sick man would die quickly, and that is no punishment."

I could not hold my eyes open any longer; oh, if I could but speak! The crafty little Sam Hawkins did not put our case very convincingly; I would have spoken differently. As I was feebly thinking this, Sam said to the young Apache chief: "We have told you clearly what our part was in this affair. Your braves would have been tortured, but Old Shatterhand prevented it by fighting Metan-Akva and conquering him. He risked his life for you, and as a reward he is to be tortured."

"You have proved nothing to me, and the whole story is a lie."

"Ask Tangua, the chief; he is in your hands."

"I have asked him, and he says you lie. Old Shatterhand did not kill Metan-Akva; he was slain by our warriors in the attack."

"That is outrageous. Tangua knows we befriended you and got the best of him, and now he wants to be revenged."

"He has sworn by the Great Spirit, and I believe him, not you. I say to you, as I have just said to Old Shatterhand, if you had been honest with me I might have pleaded for you. Kleki-Petrah, who was our father, friend, and teacher, showed me the beauty of peace and gentleness. I do not seek blood, and my father, the chief, does as I desire. Therefore we have not killed one of the Kiowas whom we captured, and they will pay us for the wrong done us, not with their lives, but with horses, weapons, skins, and vessels. Rattler is Kleki-Petrah's murderer, and must die."

Sam answered this, the longest speech I had heard from the silent Winnetou, very briefly: "We can't say we were your enemies when we are your friends."

"Silence!" said Winnetou sternly. "I see that you will die with this lie on your lips. We have allowed you more liberty than the other prisoners that you might attend Old Shatterhand. You are not worth such consideration, and henceforth you shall be more restrained. The sick man needs you no longer, and you must come with me."

"Don't say that, don't say that, Winnetou," cried Sam in horror. "I can't leave Old Shatterhand."

"You must if I command it," said the young chief. "I will not hear a word. Will you come with me, or shall my braves bind you and take you away?"

"We are in your power, and must obey. When shall we see Old Shatterhand again?"

"On the day of his death and yours."

"Not before?"

"No."

"Then let us say good-by now, before we follow you."

He grasped my hands, and I felt his beard on my face as he kissed my brow. Stone and Parker did the same, and then they went away with Winnetou.

I lay a long time alone, till the Apaches came and carried me I knew not where, for I was too weak to see, and then I was left alone again, and slept. When I awoke I could open my eyes and move my tongue a little, and was far less weak than before. I found to my surprise that I lay in the furthest corner of a large, square room, built of stone, which received its light from an opening on one side which served as door. The skins of grizzly bears had been piled on top of one another to make a comfortable bed, and I was covered with a beautifully embroidered Indian blanket. In the corner by the door sat two Indian women, one old, the other young. Like all Indian women after they are past their youth, the former was ugly, bent, and seamed by the hard work that falls on the squaws when the braves are on the war-path or hunting. But the younger was very beautiful, so much so that she would have attracted attention in any civilized society. She wore a long, light blue garment, gathered about the neck, and held around the waist by a girdle of rattlesnake-skin. Her only ornament was her long, splendid hair, which fell below her hips in two heavy black braids. It resembled Winnetou's, and the girl looked like him. She had the same velvety black eyes, which were half concealed by long, dark lashes, and there was no trace in her, nor in him, of the high cheek-bones of the Indian; her soft oval cheeks curved into a chin with a mischievous dimple. She spoke softly to the old woman, not to awaken me, and as her pretty, red lips parted in a laugh, her even, white teeth flashed between them. Her delicate nose was rather of Grecian than of Indian type, and her skin was a light copper bronze, with a silvery tint. This maiden looked about eighteen years old, and was, I felt sure, the sister of Winnetou.

I moved, and the maiden looked up from her work, rose, and came over to me. "You are awake," she said, in perfectly good English to my surprise. "Is there anything you would like?" I opened my mouth, but closed it again, realizing that I could not speak. However, I had been able to move by an effort; perhaps I could speak if I tried. I made a great effort, and said: "Yes—I—want—much."

I was delighted to hear my own voice after more than three weeks' silence, though the words came indistinctly and painfully.

"Speak slowly or by signs," said the young girl. "Nscho-Tschi sees that speech is painful to you."

"Is Nscho-Tschi your name?"

"Yes."

"It is fitting; you are like a lovely spring day when the first, sweetest flowers of the year are blooming."

Nscho-Tschi means "Fair Day," and she blushed a little at my compliment.

"Tell me what you desire," she said.

"Tell me first why you are here."

"My brother Winnetou commanded me to nurse you."

"You are very like that brave young warrior."

"You wanted to kill him." These words were said half as a question, half as a statement, while she looked searchingly into my eyes, as if she would read my very soul.

"Never!" I said emphatically.

"He does not believe that, and considers you his enemy. You have twice struck down him whom no one has conquered."

"Once to save his life; once to save my own. I loved him from the moment I first saw him."

Again she looked long at me, then she said: "He does not believe you, and I am his sister. Does your mouth pain?"

"Not now."

"Can you swallow?"

"I can try. Will you give me a drink of water?"

"Yes, and some to bathe in; we will bring it to you."

She went away with the old woman, leaving me to

wonder why Winnetou, who considered me his enemy and utterly refused to credit any assurance to the contrary, should send me his own sister as nurse.

After a time Fair Day came back with the older woman. The former carried a vessel of brown clay, such as the Pueblo Indians use, filled with fresh water. She thought me still too weak to drink without assistance, and held it to my lips herself. It was dreadfully painful to me to swallow, but it must be done. I drank in little mouthfuls and with long rests between, until the vessel was quite empty. How it refreshed me! Nscho-Tschi saw it, and said: "That has done you good. By and by I will bring you something else, for you must be hungry, too. Now will you bathe?"

The old woman brought me a gourd of water, and set it before me, with a towel of fine white flax. I tried to use them, but was too weak. My fair young nurse dipped the cloth in the water and bathed the face and hands of the supposed enemy of her father and brother.

When she had finished, she asked me with a soft little pitying laugh: "Were you always so thin?"

I felt my cheeks, and said: "I was never thin."

"Look at yourself in the water."

I looked into the gourd, and shrank back shocked, for the head of a skeleton seemed to look up at me.

"What a miracle that I am alive!" I cried.

"So Winnetou says. You have even borne the long ride here. The Great Spirit has given you an extraordinarily strong body, for few others thus wounded could have endured a journey of five days."

"Five days! Where are we?"

"In our pueblo, at Rio Pecos."

"And are the Kiowas here, too?"

"Yes. They really ought to die; any other tribe would torture them, but the good Kleki-Petrah taught us to be merciful, so they are to pay a ransom and go home."

"And my three comrades?"

"They are bound, and are in a room like this. They are well cared for, because he who is to die by torture must be strong to endure or it is no punishment."

"And are they really to die?"

"Yes."

"And I?"

"You, too."

"Will Winnetou come to me?"

"No."

"But I have something important to say to him."

"He will not hear it. Yet if you will tell me what it is, perhaps he will let me tell him about it."

"No, thank you. I could tell you perfectly well; but if he is too proud to come to me, I have a pride of my own, and will send him no messages."

"You will not see him till the day of your death. We will leave you now. If you need anything, call us; we shall hear, and will come to you."

She gave me a little willow whistle, and then went away with the old squaw.

My young nurse attended me faithfully every day; fed me savory broths and porridges from a wooden spoon, kneeling at my bedside, and nourishing me like a helpless child. Day by day I grew stronger under this care, though for a long time it hurt me dreadfully to eat. I tried to keep down all expression of pain, but in spite of myself the water would stand in my eyes when I swallowed. Nscho-Tschi saw this, and Indian-like admired silent endurance of pain.

"It is a pity," she said suddenly one day, "that you were born a lying pale-face, and not an Apache."

"I do not lie; I never lie, as you will learn later."

"I should be glad to think so, but Kleki-Petrah was the only pale-face in whom truth dwelt. You murdered him, and must die, and be buried with him."

I felt sure that I should not die, for I had incontrovertible proof of our innocence in the lock of hair which I had cut from Winnetou's head when I freed him. But had I it still? Had it not been taken from me? I searched my pockets, and found everything as I had left it; nothing had been taken from me but my weapons. I took out my box of papers, and found Winnetou's hair safely folded between them. I laid it back with a happy heart; possessing this I had no fear of dying.

I smiled at the beautiful Indian girl quite cheerfully, and said: "The sweet Fair Day will see that I shall live on many days."

She shook her head. "You are condemned by a council of the elders," she said.

"They will decide otherwise when they hear that I am innocent."

"They will not believe it."

"They must, for I can prove it."

"Oh, prove it, prove it!" she cried. "Nscho-Tschi

would be glad indeed if she could know you were no liar and traitor. Tell me your proof, or give it to me, and let me take it to Winnetou."

"Let him come to me to learn what it is."

"He will not do that."

"Nor will I send to him. I am not accustomed to sue for friendship, nor send messengers to one who can come to me."

"How unrelenting you warriors are! I should have been so glad to have brought you Winnetou's forgiveness."

"I do not need to be forgiven, for I have done no wrong. But I would ask a favor of you. In case you see Sam Hawkins, tell him to feel no anxiety, for as soon as I am well we shall be free again."

"Do not think that; this hope will never be fulfilled."

"It is not hope, but certainty; later on Fair Day will tell me I was right." The tone in which I spoke was so confident that she gave up contradicting me, and went away without another word.

I improved steadily; the skeleton took on the flesh and muscles of a living man, and the wound in my mouth healed. Nscho-Tschi remained always the same, kindly careful, yet sure that death was daily drawing nearer me. I noticed after a while that when she thought herself unobserved her eyes rested on me with a sorrowful, questioning look; she seemed to be beginning to pity me. I had thought her heartless, but had wronged her. At last, one beautiful, sunny morning in late autumn Nscho-Tschi brought my breakfast, and sat beside me, instead of keeping at a distance as she had done since

NURSED TO HEALTH FOR A CRUEL FATE. 153

I was able to move about and had almost completely regained my strength. Her eyes were moist and rested on me tenderly, and at last two tears rolled down her cheeks.

"You are crying," I said. "What has happened?"

"The Kiowas are going home; their ransom has come, and now they go."

"And that grieves you so? You must have indeed become good friends."

"You do not know of what you speak, nor suspect what lies before you. The farewell of the Kiowas is to be celebrated by your torture and that of your three white brothers."

I had been expecting this, and did not shrink as I heard it. I ate my breakfast quietly, wondering what would happen before the sun went down—possibly, in spite of my fancied security, the last sun I should look upon. I gave the dish back to Fair Day, who took it, no longer able to keep back her tears.

"This is the last time I shall speak to you," she said. "Farewell. You are called Old Shatterhand, and are a strong warrior. Be strong when they torture you. Nscho-Tschi is sore distressed by your death, but she will rejoice if you show no signs of pain and lock your groans in your own breast. Give me this happiness, and die like a hero."

With this prayer she went away, and I watched her through the open door. Then I threw myself on the bed and waited, long, anxious hours, till mid-day. At last I heard the tramp of many feet, and Winnetou entered, followed by five Apaches. He looked at me long and searchingly. "Do you remember when you were to see me again?" he asked.

"On the day of my death."

"You have said it. That day has come. Rise; you must be bound."

It would have been madness to attempt resistance, for there were six Indians against me. I rose and they tied my hands together. Then two thongs were put around my ankles, so that I could take short steps, but could not jump or run. I was then led out to the platform which ran around the pueblo house, and from which a ladder led to the ground. We descended slowly from round to round, three Indians ahead, three behind, I in the middle. On every platform stood women and children, who gazed at me in silence and then came down and fell in behind us. All the Indians of the village, numbering several hundred, were gathering to see us die.

CHAPTER XIV.

ON TRIAL FOR LIFE.

THE procession which was escorting me to torture passed on in silence, its numbers augmenting as we went. I saw that the pueblo lay in a hollow at one side of the broad valley of the Rio Pecos, into which we turned. The Indians formed a half-circle, inside of which, next the children, sat the women and maidens, among whom I saw Nscho-Tschi, whose eyes rarely wandered from my face through the following trial. My three comrades were already on the scene when I arrived, and showed that they had been well cared for during our imprisonment. The expression of faithful, loving old Sam's face was divided between irrepressible joy at seeing me again, and sorrow at the horrible circumstances in which we met to part forever.

"Ah, my dear boy," he cried, "here you come, too. It's a dreadful, very dreadful operation we're to undergo; I don't believe we can stand it. Very few live through the torture, but if we do I imagine we're to be burned."

"Have you no hope of deliverance, Sam?"

"I don't see where it's to come from. I have been racking my brains for a week, but I haven't found the least suggestion. We've been stuck in a dark stone hole of a room, tied fast and well guarded—no earthly chance to get away. How have you fared?"

"Very well."

"I believe it. You've been fattened like a Martinmas goose, and for the same reason. No, I see no deliverance for us, and the only thing to do is to die bravely. You may believe me or not, but I feel neither fear nor anxiety, though I know by night there will be nothing left of us on earth but four little handfuls of ashes."

"Possibly; but I haven't lost hope. I believe that at the end of this threatening day we shall find ourselves all right."

"Is there any foundation for your hope?"

"Yes; a lock of hair."

"A lock of hair!" he repeated in amazement. "Hair! What on earth do you mean? Has some lovely maiden in the East sent you her locks to present to the Apaches?"

"No; this is a man's hair."

He looked at me as if he doubted my sanity, shook his head, and said: "My dear young friend, you're really not right in your head. Your wound has knocked something out of place there, for I must say I do not see how a lock of hair can save us from torture."

"No, but you will see; we'll be free before the torture begins."

No one prevented our talking together. Winnetou and his father and Tangua were discussing something with the Apaches who had brought me hither, and paid no attention to us. But now Intschu-Tschuna turned around, and said in a voice plainly audible to all: "My red brothers, sisters, and children, and also the braves of the Kiowa tribe, hear me." He paused till he saw that he had every one's attention, and then continued: "The pale-faces are the enemies of the red man, and only seldom is there one whose eyes look upon us in friendship. The noblest of these few good white men came to the Apaches to be their friend and father. Therefore we gave him the name of Kleki-Petrah [*White Father*]. My brothers and sisters all knew and loved him; let them proclaim it."

"How!" arose as with one voice from the entire circle. Then the chief continued in a long and impressive speech to set forth the story of Kleki-Petrah's murder, and the attempt of the white men to build a railroad through the Indians' lands. It was a speech establishing our guilt and pointing to our death, and was interrupted at intervals by the acclaiming chorus of "How!" from the tribe.

"At the hands of any other Indians," Intschu-Tschuna said, "who knew what we know of these men, they would be given over to torture at once; but we will be obedient to the teaching of our White Father, and be a just judge; we will not condemn our enemies unheard, but they shall be convicted out of their own mouths. You have heard," he continued, turning to Sam, "what I have said. You shall tell us the truth; answer the questions I will put to you. You were with the white men who measured for the road of the fire-steed?"

"Yes, but we three did not measure your land; we

were there only to protect those who did. And as to the fourth, who is called Old Shatter—"

"Silence!" the chief interrupted. "You shall only answer my questions, and speak no further. You belong to these pale-faces? Answer yes or no."

"Yes."

"And Old Shatterhand measured with them?"

"Yes," replied Sam reluctantly.

"And you protected these people?"

"Yes."

"Then are you more guilty than they, for he who protects a thief deserves double punishment. Rattler, the murderer, was your companion?"

"Yes, but he was no friend of ours; he—"

"Silence, dog! You are only to tell me what I wish to know; if you speak beyond your brief answer you shall be whipped. You delivered us into the hands of our enemies, the Kiowas?"

"No."

"That is a lie."

"It is the truth."

"Did you not spend a whole night spying on us? Is that true or false?"

"It is true."

"And you led the pale-faces to the water to entrap us, and hid the Kiowas in the woods where they could fall upon us?"

"Yes, I did, but—"

"Silence! I want short answers and no long speech. That night and the next day we lost sixteen warriors, and they, putting aside the blood and suffering of the wounded, must be avenged. You must die; you have no claim to pity or mercy."

"We don't want mercy; we want justice," Sam interrupted.

"Will you be silent, dog?" thundered the chief. "I am through with you. But since you speak of justice, Tangua, the Kiowa chief, may testify. Are these palefaces our friends?"

"No," said the Kiowa, evidently rejoicing that things were going so badly for us. "No; they begged me to kill you, to kill you all."

This was too much for me. I broke the silence around us, crying: "That is such a shameless lie that I would knock you down if my hands were free."

"Dog!" he shrieked, "I will knock you down."

He raised his fist, but I said: "Strike, if you are not ashamed to strike a man who cannot defend himself. You have been talking here of justice, and letting us testify. Is that justice when a man can only say what you have made up your mind he shall say? How can we testify if we are to be whipped for speaking one word more than you want to hear? Intschu-Tschuna is an unjust judge; he puts the questions so that our answers must prove us guilty, allowing us to give no other, and when we would speak the truth which would deliver us, prevents us with abuse. We don't care for such justice. We'd rather you began the torture. You won't hear a sigh from us."

"Uff! uff!" I heard a woman's voice cry, and knew it was Winnetou's sister.

"Uff! uff!" cried many Apaches round her, for

courage is what Indians most respect, and they praise it even in an enemy.

I continued: "When I first saw Intschu-Tschuna and Winnetou I said to myself they were brave men and just ones, whom I could love and honor. But I was mistaken; they are no better than others, for they listen to the voice of a liar and will not hear a word of truth. Sam Hawkins has allowed himself to be silenced, but I do not care for your threats, and despise a man who oppresses a prisoner only because he is helpless. If I were free I'd talk to you differently."

"Dog! You dare to call me a liar!" cried Tangua. "I'll break your bones!"

He raised his gun to strike me, but Winnetou sprang forward, caught it, and cried: "The Kiowa chief must be quiet. Old Shatterhand has spoken boldly, but I agree with him. Intschu-Tschuna, my father, the chief of all the Apaches, may allow him to say all that he has to say."

Tangua had to obey, and Intschu-Tschuna granted his son's request.

He came near me, and said: "Old Shatterhand is like a bird of prey, that still rends though he is caged. Did you not knock Winnetou down twice? Have you not even struck me with your fist?"

"Did I do it willingly? Did you not force me to it?" I demanded.

"Forced you?" he repeated, amazed.

"Certainly. Your warriors would not listen to a word from us; they attacked us so fiercely that we had to defend ourselves; but ask them if we wounded them, though we might have killed them. Then when you came up and attacked me, you would not listen to me either; I had to defend myself, and I might have shot or stabbed you, but I knocked you down because I was your friend and would not do you real harm. Then came Tangua, the Kiowa chief, and wanted to take your scalp, and because I would not let him he attacked me, and I conquered him. Then—"

"This miserable coyote lies as if he had a hundred tongues," cried Tangua.

"Are they really lies?" asked Winnetou.

"Yes; I hope my young brother Winnetou does not doubt my word."

"I begin to; you lay senseless like my father when I came; that agrees with his story. Let Old Shatterhand continue."

"I had fought Tangua," I resumed, "to save Intschu-Tschuna when Winnetou came up. I did not see him, and he gave me a blow with his gun, fortunately not on the head, but on the shoulder. He then wounded me through the tongue, and I could not speak, or I would have told him that I would be his friend and brother, for I loved him. I was badly hurt, and my arm lamed, but I fought him, and he lay unconscious before me like Tangua and Intschu-Tschuna. I could have killed both the Apache chiefs; did I do so?"

"You would have done so, but an Apache came up and struck you down with a tomahawk," answered Intschu-Tschuna. "I admit there is something in your words that almost awakens faith in them, but when you first knocked down my son Winnetou you were not forced to do so."

"Indeed I was. We wanted to save you and him. You are brave men, and would have defended yourselves from the Kiowas, and you would have been wounded or killed. We wanted to prevent this, so I knocked Winnetou down, and you were overpowered by my friends."

"Lies, nothing but lies," cried Tangua. "I came up as he knocked you down; it was he, not I, that would have taken your scalp. I would have stopped him, but he struck me with that hand in which a great, wicked spirit dwells and nothing can stand against it."

I turned on him, and said threateningly: "I spared you, because I want to shed no man's blood; but if ever I fight you again, it will be with weapons and not my fist, and you shall not get off so easily; mark that."

"You fight me!" he jeered. "We will burn you, and scatter your ashes to the four winds."

"I think not; I shall be free sooner than you think, and demand a reckoning from you."

"You shall have it, I promise you; and I wish your words might be fulfilled that I might crush you."

Intschu-Tschuna put an end to this little interlude by saying to me: "Old Shatterhand is very bold if he thinks to be free. He has only made statements, but has not proved them. Have you anything more to say?"

"Perhaps later; not now."

"Say it now, for later you can say nothing."

"I will be silent now, for I want to see what you decide in regard to us. If I speak later, you will see that

Old Shatterhand is not a man whose word is to be despised."

Intschu-Tschuna turned from us, and nodded to certain old warriors, who left the circle and gathered around him for consultation, while Tangua of course used every effort to turn the decision as he wished. The conference lasted but a short time; the old braves came back to their places in the circle, and Intschu-Tschuna announced in a loud voice: "Hear, ye warriors of the Apaches and Kiowas, what has been determined for these four pale-faces bound here. It had been previously decided in a council of the elders that we should drive them into the water and let them fight each other, and finally we would burn them. But Old Shatterhand, the youngest of them, has spoken words which have found favor with the wisdom of the elders. They deserve death, but it seems they intended less wickedness than we believed. So we have withdrawn our first sentence, and will let the Great Spirit decide between us."

He paused for a moment, and Sam said to me: "Gracious! this is interesting, very much so. Do you know what he means?"

"I suppose a duel, an appeal to arms; don't you think so?"

"Yes, but between whom?"

The chief, continuing, answered Sam's question. "The pale-face called Old Shatterhand seems to be the foremost of them, so the decision shall be entrusted to him. He shall be opposed by the one on our side whose rank is highest; this is I, Intschu-Tschuna, the chief of the Apaches."

"The mischief! He and you!" whispered Sam in the greatest amazement.

"Uff! uff! uff!" echoed through the Apache ranks, for they, too, wondered that he should fight with me when he could so easily have appointed another to the task; but his next words explained the reason for this. "The honor of Intschu-Tschuna and Winnetou has been sorely injured," continued the chief, "they having been knocked down by the fist of this pale-face. They must wipe out this stain by fighting him. Winnetou must give way to me, for I am older, and to me belongs the right of killing Old Shatterhand."

"You may be glad," whispered Sam, "for your death will be quicker than ours."

Intschu-Tschuna spoke again: "We will unbind Old Shatterhand, and he shall go into the river to swim across it, but he shall take no weapon. I will follow him with a tomahawk. If Old Shatterhand can get across, and reach that cedar standing there in the plain, he is saved, and his comrades are free; they can go where they will. But if I kill him before he reaches the cedar they, too, must die, but not by torture; they shall be shot. Let all the braves signify that they hear my words and agree with them."

"How!" rose the answer in concert.

It may be imagined how excited they were at this announcement; Sam, Dick, and Will more than I.

"These fellows have chosen badly; because you are our superior it doesn't follow that you know how to swim. What nonsense! Their real reason is that you're a tenderfoot. I should have taken this; I'd have shown him that Sam Hawkins can go through the water like a trout. But you! Consider, my dear young friend, that not only your life but our lives hang on this; if you fail I can never speak another word to you."

"Don't worry, my dear Sam; I'll do what I can. I don't think for a moment the Indians have any underhand reason for choosing me. I am sure, too, I can save you more easily than you could have saved us."

"Well, I hope so. And it's for life or death. You mustn't spare Intschu-Tschuna; never think of doing that."

"We'll see."

"That's no answer; there's nothing to see. If you spare him, you're lost, and we with you. These redskins can throw a tomahawk a hundred feet away and cut off your fingers. You'll get it in the back or head before you can get over, no matter how well you swim."

"I know, my dear Sam, and I know, too, that a thimbleful of wit is worth more than a barrelful of mere strength."

"Wit! What good is that against a well-aimed tomahawk?"

"It helps, Sam, it helps; and I have a plan. Remember this: If I drown we are saved."

I said this hastily, for the three chiefs now came over to us. Intschu-Tschuna said: "We will now free Old Shatterhand, but he need not think he can escape, for more than a hundred will follow him to the water's edge."

"It would never occur to me," I said, "for, if I could

get away, it would be disgraceful to desert my comrades."

I was liberated, and moved my arm to test its powers. Then I said: "It is a great honor for me to contest with the chief of the Apaches, but it is not an honor for him."

"Why not?"

"Because I am no adversary for him. I have bathed, of course, but I would not dare cross such a broad, deep river as that is."

"I am sorry to hear it; Winnetou and I are the best swimmers of the tribe, and it is no victory for us to conquer a poor swimmer."

"And you are armed, while I am not; I go, then, to my death, and my comrades must also die. When will you strike me with the tomahawk?"

"When it pleases me," he said, with the contemptuous smile of a virtuoso to an amateur.

"It may be done in the water?"

"Yes."

I tried to appear more anxious and cast down than ever.

"And can I kill you?" I asked meekly.

He gave me a look which said plainly: "Poor worm! there's no question of that." But he said: "It is a contest for life or death; you may kill me, but in case such a thing happens you must still reach the cedar."

"And I shall not be held guilty of your death?"

"No; if I kill you, your comrades must die; but if you kill me and then get to the cedar, you are free. Come."

He turned away, and I pulled off my coat and vest.

Sam cried out to me in anguish: "If you could see your face and hear the mournful tone of your voice! I am in deadly fear for you and for ourselves."

I could not answer him, for the three chiefs would have heard me; but I had acted thus to make Intschu-Tschuna feel secure and less on his guard.

"One more question," I said before I followed him. "In case we are free, shall we get back our property?"

He gave a short, impatient laugh, as if he thought this an insane question. "Yes, you shall have it," he said.

"Everything?"

"Everything."

"Even horses and guns?"

He turned on me angrily, saying: "Everything; I have said it. A crow flew beside an eagle in contest of speed, and asked what it should receive if it conquered the king of birds. If you swim as stupidly as you ask questions, I am sorry I did not give you an old squaw for an adversary."

We passed through the half-circle, which opened to make way for us. As I passed Nscho-Tschi she gave me a glance in which she bade me farewell forever. The Indians followed us, and settled down to watch the interesting spectacle which was about to begin.

CHAPTER XV.

A SWIM FOR FREEDOM.

I FULLY realized the extreme danger that I was in. No matter how fast I swam, or what curves I made, the chief's tomahawk was sure to overtake me. There was but one hope, and that was in swimming under water, and fortunately I was not the bungler I had made Intschu-Tschuna think me. But I could not trust only to swimming under water, for I should have to come up to breathe, and when I did that the tomahawk would crash into my skull. No, I should not dare come to the surface, at least where the Indians could see me. How should I manage? It was with profound gratitude to God, on whom in my heart I was calling, that I saw that the surroundings were favorable to me. We stood on an open, sandy beach; the end where the woods began again was only a little over a hundred feet away from me, and just beyond that the river made a bend which promised well, and the other end of the strip of sand was a good four hundred feet down-stream. If I sprang into the water and did not come up again, they would naturally think I was drowned, and look for my body down the stream, while my plan was to swim under water in the opposite direction. There was one spot, not far up, where the river had cut under the bank, which hung over and made an excellent refuge for a short breathing-spell. Further on the bank was wooded to the edge, and an alluvial growth seemed to meet it, which would serve perfectly for the same purpose. But before the attempt was made cunning deception was necessary. Intschu-Tschuna took off all his clothes except his light Indian breeches, stuck the tomahawk into his belt, and said: " We are ready; jump in."

" Will you let me first try how deep it is ? " I asked.

A contemptuous smile passed over his face as he called for a spear. It was brought to me, and I stuck it down in the water. To my unspeakable delight it did not touch bottom; but I acted more woe-begone and scared than before, cowering down over the water, and dabbling my foot in it like one who fears a shock if the water should touch him suddenly. I heard a contemptuous murmur behind me, and Sam's voice cried out: " For the love of Heaven, come back! I can't look on at this. Let them torture us; it's better than seeing such a figure of wretchedness before a man's eyes."

I could not help wondering what Nscho-Tschi must think of me. I straightened myself and looked around. Tangua's face was the incarnation of scorn; Winnetou's upper lip had curled till one could see his teeth—he was disgusted that he had taken my part; and his sister kept her eyes down and would no longer look at me.

" I am ready; what are you waiting for now ? In with you."

" Must it really be ? " I stammered. " Is there no other way ? "

A shout of laughter arose, above which I heard Tangua's voice crying: "Let the frog go; give him his life. No warrior can lay his hand on such a coward."

And with a low growl like an angry tiger, Intschu-Tschuna said: "In with you, or I'll split your head with my tomahawk!"

I shrank away, sat down on the river brink, put first a foot and then a leg in the water, and acted as though I was going to slide in.

"In with you!" cried Intschu-Tschuna again, and upset me by a kick in the back. I threw up my arms as if I were helpless, uttered a shriek of terror, and splashed into the water. The next moment this humbug was over. I struck bottom, held my head down, and swam up-stream as fast as I could. I heard a splash behind me: Intschu-Tschuna had jumped in. I learned afterward that he had intended to let me have some headway, and throw his tomahawk when I had almost reached the other shore. But since I had shown such cowardice he abandoned this plan, and sprang in after me quickly, intending to strike me as soon as I came up; such an idiot was to be disposed of in short order.

I reached the spot where the bank hung over the stream, and let my mouth come to the surface. No one could see me except the chief, because I was under water, and to my grateful delight he kept his eyes down-stream. I drew quick, deep breaths, and sank again to continue my way. Next I came to the alluvial woods, under which I rose again to breathe. My head was so well concealed that I ventured to remain longer at the surface, and I saw the chief lying on the water like a wild beast ready any instant to pounce on its prey.

Now the last and longest stretch lay before me to the beginning of the woods, where shrubs and undergrowth hung over the bank. This I accomplished happily, and won the bank completely covered with twigs. Now to reach the bend of the river already mentioned, go around it, and swim to the opposite bank; and this must be done most quickly of all, for there was no place after this where I could come up to breathe. " Now St. Christopher, brave ferryman, help me ! " I thought. But before I started I peered out through the bushes at those whom I had fooled. They stood shouting and questioning on the bank, while the chief still swam back and forth waiting for me, although I could not possibly have remained so long under water. I wondered whether Sam Hawkins remembered that I had said that if I were drowned we were saved.

I ran through the woods till I had left the bend of the river behind me, took to the water again, and crossed safely, thanks to being considered such a bad swimmer and afraid of the water. Yet it was a clumsy trick by which they had been fooled, for they had known enough of me before to be sure I was no coward.

I followed the woods down-stream to their end. Here, looking through the bushes, I saw to my amusement that several Indians had jumped into the stream and were poking about with their spears to find Old Shatterhand's body. I could easily have walked over to the cedar, but I did not wish to owe my victory to craft alone, but to give Intschu-Tschuna a little lesson, and

make him grateful to me. He still swam around the
same spot, for it never occurred to him to look over to
the other bank. I slipped into the water again, lay on
my back, so that my mouth and nose were above water,
and slowly propelled myself downward, paddling with
my hands. No one noticed me. When I got level with
them I stood up, treading water, and shouted: "Sam
Hawkins, Sam Hawkins, we have won, we have won!"
The Indians heard me, looked over, and what a howl
arose! No one who has ever heard such a sound will
forget it to the last day of his life. As soon as Intschu-
Tschuna espied me he swam towards me with long, bold
strokes, or rather darted towards me. I dared not wait
too long, but retreated to the bank, which I climbed,
and remained standing there.

"Quick! get to the cedar, quick!" shouted Sam
Hawkins.

There was nothing to prevent my doing so, but still
I did not move, for he was not yet dangerously near.
Then I ran swiftly towards the tree. Had I been in the
water, he could have thrown the tomahawk even at that
distance; but I was sure he would not use it till we
were on a level. The tree was three hundred feet away.
When I had made half this distance as fast as I could,
I stopped again, and looked back just as the chief came
out of the water. He pulled the tomahawk from his
belt, and ran towards me. I did not move, but as he
came dangerously close I turned as if to fly, but only
apparently. I felt sure that he would not throw the
tomahawk when I stood still, for I could then dodge it.
So I started running, stopped suddenly, and turned

around. Right! He had paused to make his throw surer, swung his weapon around his head, and, even as I turned, hurled it at me. I leaped to one side: the tomahawk flew past me, and buried itself in the sand. That was what I wanted. I ran over, drew it out, and, instead of going on to the tree, walked deliberately over to the chief. He uttered an exclamation of rage, and sprang at me like a madman.

I raised the tomahawk, and called to him: "Halt, Intschu-Tschuna! You deceived yourself in Old Shatterhand. Do you want your own weapon buried in your skull?"

He paused, and cried: "Dog! How did you escape me in the water? The wicked spirit has helped you."

"Don't you believe that. If any spirit has defended me, it is the good Manitou."

As I spoke I saw a secret determination light his eyes as he watched me, and I said warningly: "You mean to surprise and attack me; I see it. Don't do it, for it would be your death. I will do you no harm, for I really care for you and Winnetou; but if you attack, I must defend myself. You know that I am stronger than you without a weapon, and I have your tomahawk. Be wise, and—"

I could say no more. His wrath mastered him beyond control of his reason. He threw himself towards me with hands outstretched like claws. He thought he had me, but I slipped aside, and the force of his own weight threw him down. Instantly I was over him; putting my left knee on one arm, my right on the other, I held him with the left hand by the throat, swung the tomahawk, and cried: "Intschu-Tschuna, do you ask for mercy?"

"No."

"Then I'll split your head."

"Kill me, you dog!" he gasped, struggling to get away.

"No, you are Winnetou's father, and shall live; but I must make you take a nap for a little while. You leave me no choice."

I struck his head with the flat side of the tomahawk— a severe blow; his limbs drew up convulsively, and then stretched out at full length. It looked from where the Indians stood as though I had killed him, and again I heard that awful howl.

I bound the chief's arms down to his side with his belt, dragged him over to the cedar, and laid him at its foot. I had to reach the tree, under the conditions laid down, to complete the work and win our freedom. Then I left Intschu-Tschuna lying there, and ran quickly back to the bank, for three Indians had thrown themselves into the stream and were swimming over, Winnetou at their head. In case they did not keep their word this was too many, so I called to them as I reached the river: "Your chief lives; I have done him no harm; but if you come here I will kill you. Only Winnetou shall cross, for I wish to speak to him." They paid no attention to these words, but Winnetou rose in the water where they could all see him, and uttered a word which I did not understand. They obeyed it, turned back, and he came on alone. I waited for him at the water's edge, and as he emerged from it said: "It is well they turned back, for it would have proved dangerous to your father to have allowed them to come."

"You have slain him with the tomahawk."

"No; he forced me to strike him unconscious, because he would not give in."

"And you could have killed him; he was in your hands."

"I would not willingly kill an enemy; certainly not a man I like and who is Winnetou's father. Here is his tomahawk. You shall decide whether or not I have conquered and the promise to me and my comrades shall be fulfilled."

He took the tomahawk which I held out to him, and regarded me long and steadily. His eyes grew milder and milder; their expression changing into one of amazement, and at last he said: "What kind of a man is Old Shatterhand? who can understand him?"

"You will learn to understand me."

"You give me this weapon, not knowing whether we will keep our word or not, yet you could defend yourself with it. Do you know you have delivered yourself into my hands?"

"Pshaw! I'm not afraid, for in any case I have my hands, and Winnetou is no liar, but a noble warrior, whose word will never be broken."

He stretched out his hand to me, and replied: "You are right; you are free, and the other pale-faces also, except the man called Rattler. You have confidence in me; would I could have confidence in you!"

"You will yet trust me as much as I trust you; wait only a little while. Now come to your father."

"Yes, come; when Old Shatterhand strikes death may follow, even when he does not intend it."

We went over to the chief. Winnetou examined him, and then said: "He lives, and will come to himself later with an aching head. I must not stay here, but I will send some men over to him. My brother Old Shatterhand may come with me."

This was the first time he had called me "my brother." How often I heard him say it afterward, and how sincere, true, and faithful he was saying it!

We turned back, and swam across the river. The Indians stood on the opposite bank and saw us coming; they could perceive the difference in Winnetou's manner to me, and must have recognized the fact that I was not what they supposed, either in the wrong done to them, or in cowardice.

As we reached the bank Winnetou took me by the hand and said: "Old Shatterhand has conquered; he and his three comrades are free."

"Uff! uff! uff!" cried the Apaches, while Tangua stood looking at us darkly.

Winnetou strode past him without looking at him, and led me to the stakes to which my three comrades were bound.

"Hallelujah!" cried Sam. "We are saved! Man, youngster, tenderfoot, how did you do it?"

Winnetou gave me his knife. "Cut their bonds," he said. "You deserve to do it yourself."

I did so. As soon as they were free they threw themselves on me, and took me in their arms, hugging me till I was actually hurt. Sam even kissed my hand, with tears dropping into his beard. "My dear boy," he said, "if ever I forget you, may the first grizzly I meet devour me skin and hair! How did you do this? You were so afraid of the water, and everybody thought you were drowned."

"Did I not tell you that if I were drowned we were saved?"

"Did Old Shatterhand say this before the contest?" asked Winnetou. "Was it then all planned beforehand?"

"Yes," I nodded.

"My brother knew what he would do. My brother is not only as strong as a bear, but as cunning as the fox of the prairie. Whoso is his enemy must be on his guard."

"And is Winnetou such an enemy?"

"I was, but am no longer."

"So you no more believe Tangua, the liar, but me?"

Again he looked at me long and searchingly as before, extended his hand, and said: "Your eyes are good eyes, and there is no dishonesty in your face. I believe you."

I had resumed my discarded clothing, and took my tin box from the pocket of my hunting-jacket, and said: "Therein has my brother Winnetou done me justice; I will prove it to him. Perhaps he may know what this is."

I unrolled the lock of hair, and held it up before him. He put out his hand to take it, stopped short, and stepped back, completely amazed, crying: "It is my own hair. Who gave you this?"

"Intschu-Tschuna said this morning in his address

that the Great Spirit had sent you an unknown deliverer when you were a prisoner in the hands of the Kiowas. Yes, he was unknown, for he dared not let the Kiowas see him; but now there is no longer need of his concealing himself. You may truly believe that I was not your foe, but your friend."

"You—you—it is you who freed us?" he gasped, more and more overcome, he who never betrayed surprise. "Then we owe you not only our freedom but our lives."

He took me by the hand, and drew me to the place where his sister stood watching us intently. He led me before her, and said: "Nscho-Tschi, see here the brave warrior who secretly freed our father and me when we were bound to the trees by the Kiowas. Let us thank him."

With these words he drew me to him, and kissed me on each cheek. She held out her hand to me, saying only: "Forgive."

She was to thank me, but instead begged for forgiveness. But I understood her; she had been secretly unjust to me; as my nurse she should have known me better than the others, yet she, too, had doubted me, and taken me for a miserable coward. She felt that it was more important to make this right than to thank me as Winnetou wished.

I pressed her hand and said: "Nscho-Tschi will remember all I said to her; now it is fulfilled. Will my sister believe me now?"

Fair Day smiled on me, and said simply: "I believe my white brother."

I went back to explain to my three friends the mystery of the lock of hair, and tell them that it was I who had freed the chiefs, while Winnetou went to seek his father. Presently we saw them returning, and went to meet them. Intschu-Tschuna looked at me with the same searching gaze his son had given me, then he said: "Winnetou has told me all; you are free, and will forgive us. You are a mighty and cunning warrior, and will conquer many foes. He who is wise will be your friend. Will you smoke the calumet of peace with us?"

"Yes, I would gladly be your friend and brother."

"Then come with me and Nscho-Tschi, my daughter, to the pueblo. I will give my conqueror a dwelling worthy of him. Winnetou, stay here to make the arrangements you know of."

We went back with him and Nscho-Tschi as free men to the pueblo which we had quitted prisoners on our way to death.

CHAPTER XVI.

TANGUA'S PUNISHMENT.

As we approached the pueblo I saw for the first time what an imposing stone structure it was. The American savage has not been supposed to have had ability to build, but men who could raise such masses of stone as the southwestern Indians have put into their pyramidal pueblos, and knew how to fasten them securely with such insufficient tools as they possessed, surely did not stand in the lowest ranks of intelligence or knowledge of architecture. And though it is said with truth that these Indians once possessed knowledge which their descendants have lost, it must be remembered that if time and opportunity for advancement be denied them they must inevitably deteriorate, and their present inferiority proves rather the oppression of the white man than the incapacity of the red man.

We climbed to the raised platform behind which lay the best apartments of the pueblo. There Intschu-Tschuna dwelt with his children, and there apartments were given us also. Mine was a large room, which like my first one had no window, receiving its light only through the door, but this was so broad and high that there was plenty of light. The room was bare, but Nscho-Tschi furnished it quickly with skins, covers, and ornaments, so that I felt at home at once. Hawkins, Stone, and Parker were given a pleasant room together.

When the "guest-chamber" had been prepared, and I had taken possession of it, Fair Day brought me a beautifully carved pipe of peace with tobacco. She filled it herself, lighted it, and as I drew the first whiff said: "My father Intschu-Tschuna sends you this pipe. He took the clay for it himself from the sacred stone quarry, and I cut it. No man has ever had it between his lips, and we beg you to accept it for your own, and remember us when you smoke it."

"Your goodness is great," I said. "I feel ashamed that I can make no gift in return."

"You have already given us so much that we cannot thank you for it; the lives of Intschu-Tschuna and Winnetou were in your hands, and you spared them, and to-day again you might have killed the chief and you did not do so. Therefore our hearts turn to you, and if you will you shall be our brother."

"If that may be, then my dearest wish will be fulfilled. Intschu-Tschuna is a renowned warrior, and I have loved Winnetou from the first moment that I saw him. It would not only be a great honor but a great joy to be the brother of such men; I only wish that my comrades could share it."

"If they will, they shall be treated as if they had been born Apaches."

"We thank you for this. So you carved the head of this pipe yourself? How skilful your hands are!"

She blushed over this praise, and said: "I know that the women and daughters of the pale-faces are far more skilful than we. Now I will go, and bring you something else."

She disappeared, and returned with my revolver, my knife, and everything else that had been in my pockets, with nothing missing or injured.

"And how about our horses?" I asked.

"They are all here; you shall ride yours again, and Hawkins is to have his Nancy."

"So you know the mule's name?"

"Yes, and the name of the old gun which he calls his 'Liddy.' When you were ill I used to go to him every day to tell him you were progressing. He is a funny man, but a good hunter."

"Yes, and he is far more than that. He is a true, self-sacrificing comrade, whom you can't help loving. Now will you answer a question truthfully?"

"Nscho-Tschi does not lie," she replied, simply and proudly, "and least of all would I lie to you."

"Then why did your warriors leave the contents of my pockets untouched when they took everything away from my comrades and the Kiowas?"

"Because my brother Winnetou ordered it so."

"And do you know why he gave such an order?"

"Because he liked you."

"Although he considered me his enemy?"

"Yes. You said a little while ago that you liked him from the moment you first saw him; he had a similar feeling for you. It grieved him to be forced to hold you his enemy, and not only an enemy—" She stopped, evidently because what she was going to say would have wounded me.

"Say on," I said.

She shook her head.

"Then I'll finish for you. It did not grieve him so much to consider me his enemy, for one can respect an enemy, but to consider me a liar, a treacherous, false man. Is that it?"

"You have said it."

"Never mind; I think he knows now he was mistaken. What about Rattler?"

"He will be tortured in a little while."

"And why was I not told?"

"Winnetou would have it so; he thought your eyes could not see nor your ears hear his agony."

"I've no doubt he is right; but if I can bring about what I desire I can bear it. In any case I must be there. What torture is intended for him?"

"Everything possible. He is the worst pale-face that the Apaches have ever captured. He killed our White Father, whom we loved and honored, and for no reason; therefore he must die by every agony which we know, slow and long-continued."

"That must not be; it is inhuman."

"He deserves it."

"And can you look at it?"

"Yes."

"You, a maiden!"

She dropped her long lashes, and then raised her eyes to mine. "Your women are not more tender-hearted than we. They do cruel things only for their own pleasure, kill little birds for their feathers, and are not always gentle; Kleki-Petrah has told me of them. Our ways are not your ways, but a woman's heart is everywhere the same, whatever the color of her skin. The white men have not taught the Indian kindness, truth, or justice. I can look on the punishment of a man who, in murdering Kleki-Petrah, has given us pain greater than his. But I ask you not to come to see Rattler tortured, for Intschu-Tschuna and Winnetou will not be pleased if they see you coming with me."

"I will go with you none the less, and they will pardon it," I said.

We descended the ladder again, and met Winnetou when we had gone but a short distance. I had completely forgotten Tangua until that moment when I saw him standing near, and there was no mistaking how angry he was.

I went up to him, and looking him steadily in the face demanded: "Is Tangua, the Kiowa chief, a liar, or does he love truth?"

"Would you insult me?" he shrieked.

"No; I only want to know. Answer me."

"Old Shatterhand must know that I love truth," he said.

"You remember, then, what you said to me when I was bound over yonder."

"I said many things to you."

"You certainly did; but you know what I mean. If you don't I'll help your memory. You said that we should have a settlement."

"Did I say that?" he asked, elevating his brows.

"Yes, and you said further that you would be glad to fight me, for you would crush me."

"I don't remember that; Old Shatterhand must have misunderstood me."

"No; Winnetou was there and can confirm it."

"Yes," said Winnetou readily. "Tangua said he would settle with Old Shatterhand, whom he would gladly fight, for he would crush him."

"Now," I continued, "you called me a frog without courage, and tried in every way to do me harm. You've got to eat your words."

I felt that I must punish this Indian, not merely for justice' sake and the effect on the Apaches, but for the benefit of those white men whom he might meet in the future.

"My brother Old Shatterhand is right," said Winnetou. "If you do not keep your promise you will be a coward, and should be expelled from your tribe. Such things must not happen here, for no man shall reproach the Apaches with having a coward for a guest. What does the Kiowa chief intend to do?"

"I will consider it."

"For a brave warrior there is nothing to consider. Fight or be called a coward."

Tangua drew himself up, saying haughtily: "Tangua a coward! I will bury my knife in the heart of him who says it."

"I say it—I," said Winnetou coolly, "if you do not keep your word to Old Shatterhand."

"I will keep it."

"Then are you ready?"

"This moment; I long to taste his blood."

"Good! Old Shatterhand will decide the weapons, for you insulted him."

"No; I am a chief, and am greater than he."

"Let him choose," I interrupted. "It makes no difference to me what they are."

"It shall be guns, two hundred paces apart, and I will shoot first."

Winnetou shook his head. "Tangua would have all the advantages for himself," he said. "Old Shatterhand must shoot first."

"No," I said. "He shall have his way. Let him shoot once, and I once, and no more."

"No," said Tangua, "we will shoot till one falls."

"Certainly; for after my first shot you will be down."

"Boaster!"

"You will see. I could kill you, but I will not. The most severe punishment for you would be to lame you; I will break your right knee. Remember."

"Do you hear that?" he laughed. "This pale-face, whom his own friends call a greenhorn, announces beforehand where his shot shall go at two hundred paces! Braves, let us laugh at him."

He looked around invitingly, but no one laughed, and he said: "You are afraid of him, but I will show you how I mock him. Come, let us measure the paces."

While this was being done I got my gun, examined it, and found it in good condition. Both barrels were loaded, but to be sure of them I discharged and reloaded them. Sam came up, and said: "I have a hundred questions to ask you, and can't get a chance. However, there's one thing I must ask you, and that is if you're really going to shoot this fellow in the knee?"

"Yes."

"Only there?"

"That is punishment enough."

"No, it certainly is not. Such vermin ought to be stamped on. Only think of what he has been guilty, and everything has come from his having stolen the Apaches' horses in the first place. If I were in your place I would put a bullet into his head; he'll do his best to get one into yours."

"Or in my heart; I know that perfectly well."

"But he won't succeed; these Kiowas are no good at shooting."

The ground has been measured by this time, and we took our places. I was quiet as usual, but Tangua poured out a stream of abuse upon me, till Winnetou, who stood on one side between us, said: "Let the Kiowa chief be silent and pay attention. I will count three, and then he may shoot; he who shoots before the time shall have my bullet in his head."

Of course all the Indians were watching us with intense interest. They had divided into two files, to right and left of us, so that a broad path ran between them, at the end of which we stood. The deepest stillness reigned. "The chief of the Kiowas may begin," said Winnetou. "One—two—three." I stood still, presenting the entire width of my body to my antagonist. At Winnetou's first word he raised his gun, aimed carefully, and at "three" fired. The shot went over me, close to my head. No one uttered a sound.

"Now Old Shatterhand may shoot," said Winnetou. "One—two—"

"Wait," I interrupted. "I stand up fairly to the

Kiowa chief, but he has turned half around, so that the side of his face is towards me."

"I may do so," said Tangua. "Who shall forbid it? There was nothing said as to how we should stand."

"That is true, and Tangua certainly may stand as he likes. He has turned his side to me because, that being narrower than the breast, he thinks it will be harder for me to hit, but he is mistaken; I can hit him just as well. I might have shot without a word, but I'll be honorable with him. He was to have a wound only in the right knee, but now that cannot be, for if he stands with his side towards me the shot will shatter both knees. That is the only difference; he can do as he likes; I have warned him."

"Shoot with bullets and not with words," he answered, ignoring my warning.

"Now Old Shatterhand shoots," said Winnetou. "One—two—three." My bullet whistled through the air. Tangua uttered a loud shriek, dropped his gun, threw up his arms, waved them about wildly, and fell.

"Uff! uff! uff!" echoed all around, and every one ran over to see where he had been wounded. I also went over, the Indians respectfully making way for me.

"In both knees, in both knees!" I heard on all sides.

Tangua lay moaning on the ground as I came up; Winnetou knelt by him examining the wound. He saw me coming, and said: "The shot has gone just where my white brother said it should; it has broken both knees. Tangua can never again ride out to cast his eyes on the horses of another tribe."

When the wounded man saw me he began another

torrent of abuse, but I compelled him to be silent a moment, and said: "I warned you, and you would not heed the warning; you alone are to blame."

He dared not complain of the pain, for under no circumstances may an Indian do this; he bit his lip, looked sullenly around, and growled: "I am wounded, and cannot go home; I must stay with the Apaches."

Winnetou shook his head, and answered decidedly: "You will go home, for we have no room for the thief of our horses and the murderer of our braves. We have not avenged ourselves with blood, but have accepted ransom in beasts and goods; more you cannot expect. No Kiowa belongs in our pueblo."

"But I cannot ride."

"Old Shatterhand was much more severely wounded than you are, and could not ride, yet he had to come with us. Think of him often; it will be good for you. The Kiowas must leave here to-day, and those of them that we find in our domains to-morrow we will treat as they wished Old Shatterhand to be treated. I have spoken. How!"

He took me by the hand and led me away, and I knew, though he said nothing, that he was pleased with the result of this last adventure and the punishment of his treacherous foe.

CHAPTER XVII.

THE END OF RATTLER.

WINNETOU and I walked a little distance away from the Indians who were still assembling to see Rattler's torture. When we had gone beyond their hearing, Winnetou asked me gravely why I had left the pueblo.

"We came back because we heard that Rattler was soon to die; is that so?" I asked.

"Yes."

"I do not see him anywhere."

"He lies in the cart beside the body of his victim."

"I was told that he was to be tortured, and I cannot look upon such a death."

"Therefore my father, Intschu-Tschuna, took you back to the pueblo. Why did you not stay there? Why do you want to see something you cannot look upon?"

"I hope that I may be present at his death without being shocked. My religion teaches me to plead with you for Rattler."

"Your religion? Is it not his also?"

"Yes and no; he was born a Christian, but not a Catholic Christian."

"Did he keep its commandments?"

"Most certainly he did not."

"Then it is not necessary for you to observe them in regard to him. Your religion forbids murder; nevertheless he is a murderer, so the teachings of your religion are not to be applied to our treatment of him."

"I cannot be guided by what he has done; I must fulfil my duty without regard to other men's shortcomings. I beg of you, modify your decision, and let this man die a speedy death."

"What has been determined upon must be carried out."

"And is there no way to fulfil my request?"

Winnetou's eyes sought the ground; he thought earnestly for a while, then said: "There is a way, but before I tell my white brother what it is I must beg him not to use it, for it would disgrace him sorely in the eyes of our warriors."

"How would it? Is it a dishonorable action?"

"In the eyes of a red man it is. You would have to appeal to our gratitude."

"Oh, no decent man would do that."

"No. We owe you our lives. If you appeal to that fact you could force my father and me to do your will. We would hold a new council, and during it we would speak of you in such a way that our warriors must acknowledge our debt to you and grant your desire. But henceforth everything you have done for us would be valueless. Is this Rattler worth such a sacrifice?"

"Certainly not."

"My brother sees that I speak frankly to him. I know the thoughts and feelings in his heart, but my braves would never grasp them. A man who appealed to gratitude would be contemptible to them. Shall Old Shatterhand, who can become the greatest and most renowned warrior of the Apaches, be driven away from us to-day because our braves despise him?"

It was hard for me to answer; my heart bade me press my request, my common-sense forbade it. Winnetou understood the struggle within me, and said: "I will speak to Intschu-Tschuna, my father. My brother may wait here."

"Don't do anything foolish," said Sam as he left us. "You don't know how much may depend on this; maybe life itself."

"Oh, that couldn't be," I said.

"Indeed it could easily. The red man so greatly despises any one who asks a favor on the strength of what has been done for him that we actually could not stay here if you did it; and if we left here we should surely fall into the hands of the Kiowas, and there's no need of telling you what that means."

Intschu-Tschuna and Winnetou talked earnestly together for a while, then they came to us, and the former said: "Had not Kleki-Petrah told me so much of your faith, I should feel you were a man to whom it was a disgrace to talk. But I can understand your wish perfectly; though if my warriors were to hear it they would never understand, and would only despise you."

"It is not a question of my wish alone, but of Kleki-Petrah's, of whom you speak," I said.

"How is it a question of his desire?"

"He believed in this same faith which commands me to make this plea, and he died in it. His religion bade him forgive his enemies. Believe me, if he could speak he would not consent to his murderer dying such a death."

"Do you really think so?"

"I know it."

He shook his head slowly. "What kind of men are you Christians? Either you are bad, and then your wickedness is so great that no one can understand it, or else you are good, and then your goodness is equally incomprehensible."

He and his son looked at each other, and spoke together privately, but only for a moment. Then Intschu-Tschuna turned back to me and said: "This murderer was your enemy also?"

"Yes."

"And you have forgiven him?"

"Yes."

"Then hear me. We will see if there is the least, tiniest spark of goodness in him. Should we find one, we will try to do as you wish without disgracing you. Sit here and wait. If I give you a signal, come over to the murderer, and tell him to ask your pardon. If he does this, he shall die quickly."

"And may I tell him so?"

"Yes."

Intschu-Tschuna went back with Winnetou to the circle of braves, and we sat down where we were.

"I never dreamed that the chief would listen to you," said Sam Hawkins. "You must stand well with him."

"That is not the only reason; it is the influence of Kleki-Petrah, powerful though he is dead. These Indians have absorbed more real, interior Christianity than you suspect."

We looked over towards the cart wherein the doomed man lay, and saw a long box-like object, on which a man was bound.

"That is the coffin," said Sam, "made of hollow logs with wet leather drawn over them, which will be air-tight when the leather has dried. Kleki-Petrah's body has been embalmed, you know."

Not far from the head of the valley rose a cliff on which an open square had been newly made of great stones piled on top of each other, and many more stones had been gathered together around it. The man bound on the coffin was now carried to this square. It was Rattler.

"Do you know why those stones have been collected there?" asked Sam.

"To build a tomb, I suppose."

"Yes; a double tomb."

"For Rattler, too?"

"Yes; they will bury the murderer with his victim."

"Horrible! Think of being bound alive to the coffin of the man one killed, knowing that is to be one's last resting-place!"

"I really believe you are sorry for this man. I can understand your interceding for a quick death for him, but I certainly can't understand your pity for him."

The coffin was now raised so that Rattler was placed on his feet, and he was bound fast by strong ropes to the stone wall of the tomb. The Indians, men, women, and children drew near to the place, and made a half-circle around it. Profound, expectant silence reigned. Intschu-Tschuna stood before the coffin and spoke. "The Apache braves are gathered here because their people have suffered a great loss, and he who has caused it must pay for it with his life," he said. He then spoke in the figurative Indian manner of Kleki-Petrah, telling them of his character and work, and the way in which he had met his death, and concluded by announcing that it had been decided that Rattler was now to be tortured, bound as he then was to the coffin, and should be buried with his victim. Turning to me at this point, he gave me the expected signal, and we went forward and were admitted into the circle. I had been too far away before to see Rattler clearly, but now as I stood before him, wicked and godless as he was, I felt the most profound pity for the wretch. The coffin was twice the width of a man's body and over eight feet long. Rattler was fastened with his back to it, his arms behind him, and his feet stretched apart. He showed that he had suffered from hunger and thirst. A gag was in his mouth, and he could not speak; his head, too, was fastened so that he could not move it. As I came up, Intschu-Tschuna took the gag out of his mouth, and said:

"My white brother wished to speak to this murderer; now he may do so."

Rattler could see that I was free and must be on good terms with the Indians. I thought, therefore, that he would ask me to speak a good word for him; but, instead of this, as soon as the gag was removed he said to me bitterly: "What do you want of me? Get out of here! I don't want anything to do with you."

"You have heard that you were doomed to die, Rattler," I said gently. "There is no way out of that; die you must, but—"

"Get out, you dog, get out!" he shrieked, trying to spit upon me, but failing because he could not move his head.

"You must die," I continued unmoved, "but how depends upon yourself. You are to be tortured; that means long, long agony, through all this day, and perhaps to-morrow. It is horrible to think of, and I want you to escape it. At my request Intschu-Tschuna has declared that you shall die quickly if you will fulfil the condition he has made."

I waited for him to ask me what the condition was, but instead of doing so he poured out a storm of abuse upon me which could not be repeated. As soon as I could speak I said: "The condition is that you ask my pardon."

"Your pardon! I'd bite my tongue out first, and suffer all the tortures this red beast can give me."

"Remember, I did not make the condition, Rattler; it was Intschu-Tschuna who decided thus, for I don't care about your apology. Consider what awful agony lies before you, and that you can escape it all by saying the little word 'Pardon.'"

"Never, never! Get out, I tell you! I never want to see your vile face again. Go, and don't bother me."

"If I go now, it will be too late to call me back. Be sensible, and speak the one little word, I beg you."

"No, I tell you, no. Get out! Oh, if I weren't tied I'd show you the way!"

"As you please; but if you call me back I can't come. Have you any relatives I can send a message to? Any wish that I can carry out?"

"Only that you may follow me soon; nothing else."

"Then I am helpless, and can do no more except beg you, as a Christian, not to die in your sins. Ask God's pardon, if not mine; think of your crimes, and of the judgment that lies before you."

What his reply to this was I cannot repeat; his words chilled me with horror.

Intschu-Tschuna took my hand and led me away, saying: "My young white brother sees that this murderer does not deserve his intercession. He was born a Christian, and you call us heathen; but do you think a red brave would speak such words?"

I did not answer, for what could I say? Rattler's conduct was inexplicable to me; he had been so cowardly, and had shown such abject terror at the very mention of torture, and now he acted as though all the pains of the world were absolutely nothing.

"It is not courage," said Sam; "it's clear rage, nothing but rage. He thinks it's your fault that he has fallen into the Apaches' hands. He hasn't seen you since we were captured till to-day, and now he sees you free and the red men friendly to you, while he must die, and that's ground enough for him to conclude we've played some trick. But let the agony begin, and he'll sing another tune."

The Apaches did not let us wait long for the beginning of the torture. I meant to withdraw; but I had never seen anything of the kind, and decided to stay till I could look on no longer.

Several young braves came out from the rest with knives in their hands, and placed themselves about fifteen feet from Rattler. Then at a signal from the chief they began throwing their knives at him in such a way that these would not touch him, but would enter the coffin all around him. The first knife stuck in the leather at the right, the second in that at the left of his feet, and so near them that there was no space between them and the knives. The next two knives were aimed farther up, and so on until the legs were outlined by knives. Till now Rattler had kept still; but as the knives came higher and higher till his whole body was surrounded by them, he began to be afraid. As each knife whizzed through the air he uttered a cry of terror, and these cries grew shriller and shriller the higher the Indians aimed. Now the body was all framed around with knives, only the head being free. The first of the knives next thrown struck the coffin to the left of the neck, the second to the right, and they continued around the face till there was no room left for the smallest blade, when all the knives were drawn out. This was only a little introductory game, played by young lads to show they had learned to aim true and throw straight; and having shown their skill they returned to their places.

Intschu-Tschuna now called upon older youths, who were to throw at a distance of thirty feet. When the first of this band was ready, the chief went up to Rattler and, pointing to the upper part of the right arm, said: "Aim here."

The knife flew through the air, pierced the muscle, and stuck in the coffin exactly at the spot designated. Rattler uttered a howl as if he were in his last agony. The second knife went through the same spot in the other arm, and his howls redoubled. The third and fourth knives were aimed at the thigh, and entered exactly at the spot the chief indicated.

If Rattler had fancied that the Indians did not really mean to kill him, he saw now that he was mistaken. Heretofore he had uttered only single cries; now he howled unceasingly. The spectators murmured and hissed, showing their contempt in every possible way. An Indian who dies by torture acts far differently. As soon as the spectacle which is to end with his death begins he raises his death-song, in which he celebrates his own prowess and scorns those who are killing him. The greater his agony the greater the insults he heaps upon his foes, and he never lets a sigh of pain be heard. When he is dead his enemies acknowledge his glory, and bury him with all Indian honors. It is glorious for them to put such a hero to death, but it is quite different in the case of a coward who shrinks from the slightest pain and begs for mercy. There is no glory, but almost disgrace, in torturing such as he, and scarcely a warrior is willing to have any part in his end; so he is knocked in the head, or put to death in some other ignominious way. Such a coward was Rattler. His wounds were trifling so far; they cost him some pain, but they were far from being agony; nevertheless he howled as though he tasted all the pains of the lost, and kept repeating my name, begging me to come to him.

"My young white brother may go to him and ask him why he shrieks so. The knives cannot yet have given him much pain," Intschu-Tschuna said at last.

"Yes, come; come here, come!" cried Rattler. "I must speak to you."

I went, and asked him what he wanted.

"Take the knives out of my arms and legs," he whined.

"I can't do that."

"But they'll kill me; who can bear such wounds?"

"Good gracious! Is it possible you thought you'd be allowed to live?"

"You're alive."

"Yes, but I have not committed murder."

"I did not know what I did; you know I was drunk."

"The fact remains the same; you were often warned against liquor, and you knew when you took it what a beast it made you."

"You are a hard cruel man. Plead for me."

"I have done so. Ask pardon and you shall die quickly."

"Die quickly! I won't die. I must live, live, live."

"That is impossible."

"Impossible! Is there no hope?"

"None at all."

"No hope, no hope, no hope," he wailed, and began such a clamor of cries and groans that I could not stand it, and left him alone.

"Stay with me—stay with me," he shrieked. "Stand by me."

The chief interrupted him. "Stop howling, you cur. You are not worth soiling the weapons of our braves." And turning to his warriors he asked: "Which of the sons of the brave Apaches will put an end to this coward?"

No one answered.

"Will no one do it?"

Again silence.

"Uff! This murderer is not worthy to be killed by us, and he shall not be buried with Kleki-Petrah. How could such a crow appear in the Happy Hunting Grounds beside a swan? Cut him loose."

Two little boys sprang forward at a signal, drew the knives from Rattler's limbs, and cut his bonds.

"Bind his hands behind his back," continued the chief.

The boys, who could not have been more than ten years old, obeyed him, and Rattler did not make the slightest attempt at resistance. What a disgrace! I blushed to be a white man.

"Take him to the river, and push him into the water," was the next order. "If he can get to the other shore he shall be free."

Rattler uttered a cry of joy, and let the boys lead him to the river. They actually did push him in, for he had not sufficient sense of decency to jump in himself. He sank at once, but came up again quickly, and tried to advance by swimming on his back, which was not difficult though his hands were tied, for his legs were free. Would he reach the opposite bank? I could not hope that he would; he deserved to die, and if he were allowed to live the one who spared him would almost render himself guilty of the future crimes the miserable man was sure to commit. The boys stood close to the water, and watched him.

"Get guns, and shoot him in the head," said Intschu-Tschuna.

The children ran to the place where the braves had left their weapons, and each took a gun. These little fellows knew well how to handle such weapons; they knelt on the ground, and aimed at Rattler's head.

"Don't shoot; for Heaven's sake don't shoot," he cried.

The boys spoke to one another; they acted like little sportsmen in letting Rattler swim farther and farther, and the chief did not interfere, seeing they knew their business.

Suddenly their shrill, boyish voices rang out in a sharp cry, and they shot. Rattler was hit in the head, and instantly disappeared under the water. No cry of triumph arose such as Indians always utter at the death of an enemy. Such a coward was not worth breath, and their contempt was so great that not an Indian looked after his body. They let it float where it would, not even taking the trouble to make sure he was dead.

Intschu-Tschuna came to me and asked: "Is my young white brother satisfied with me?"

"Yes; I thank you."

"You have no reason to thank me. If I had not known your wish I should still have acted nearly as I did. This cur was not worthy to suffer torture. You have seen to-day the difference between brave red warriors and cowardly white men. The pale-faces are all ready for any wickedness, but when there is question of showing courage they howl like dogs that see the whip."

"The chief of the Apaches must remember that there are cowards and brave men everywhere, as there are good and bad ones."

"You are right, and I will not wound you. But no nation should think itself better than another because it is not of the same color."

CHAPTER XVIII.

TEACHING WINNETOU.

"AND now there is but one thing left to do to finish the work begun in our meeting—a happy meeting in some ways, though so tragic in others," I said to the chief as we walked slowly towards Winnetou, whom we saw approaching. "The Apache braves have only to bury Kleki-Petrah, and then all will be completed, will it not ?"

"Yes."

"May I be present with my comrades ?"

"Certainly; I should have asked you had you not made the request. You talked with Kleki-Petrah on that miserable morning while we were gone for our horses; was it an ordinary conversation ?"

"No; it was a very earnest one, and important to us both. May I tell you of what we talked ?" Winnetou had reached us as I spoke, and I turned to him with this question.

"Tell us," he said.

"While you were gone that morning Kleki-Petrah and I sat down beneath a tree. We soon discovered that we were of the same faith, and he opened his heart to me. He had gone through a great deal, and borne much, and he told me of his life. He also told me how dear you were to him, and that it was his desire to die for Winnetou. This wish the Great Spirit fulfilled but a few moments later."

" Why did he wish to die for me ? " asked Winnetou.

" Because he loved you, and also for another reason which I will explain later. His death would then be an expiation."

" As he lay dying on my heart he spoke to you in a tongue I could not understand; what was it ? "

" His mother tongue—German."

" Did he speak of me then, too ? "

" Yes."

" What did he say ? "

" He begged me to be true to you."

" Be true—to me ? You did not know me then."

" I knew you, for I had seen you; and whoever sees Winnetou must know what kind of a man stands before him. Besides, Kleki-Petrah told me of you."

" What answer did you give him ? "

" I promised to fulfil his wish."

" It was his last wish. You then became his heir. You promised him to be true to me, and you protected me, guarded me, watched over me while I pursued you as my enemy. The knife-thrust I gave you would have been fatal to another, but your stronger frame it only wounded. I am very, very guilty towards you. Be my friend."

" I have long been that."

" My brother."

" With all my heart."

" Then we will cement the bond over the grave of him who gave my soul into your care. A noble pale-face has gone from us, and even in going has given us another equally noble. My blood shall be your blood, and your blood shall be my blood; I will drink yours, and you shall drink mine. Intschu-Tschuna, the greatest chief of the Apaches, my father, will consent to this?"

Intschu-Tschuna gave us each a hand, and said in a tone that evidently came from his heart: "I consent. You shall be not merely brothers, but a single man with two bodies. How!"

Having said this the chief left us, and Winnetou and I went away together, and sat down by the bank of the broad Rio Pecos, now reddening in the setting sun. The depths of Winnetou's earnest nature had been profoundly stirred by what he had just learned of his beloved teacher's dying love and care for him. He took my hand, and held it in his own for a long time without speaking, and I had no desire to break the silence. At last Winnetou moved, sighed, and asked: "Will my brother Old Shatterhand forget that we were his enemies?"

"It is already forgotten," I replied.

"But there is one thing you cannot forgive," he said.

"What is that?"

"The insult my father gave you the day we met."

"Oh, after the murder, when he spat in my face?"

"Yes."

"Why could I not forgive that?"

"Because only blood can wash away such an insult."

"Winnetou may dismiss all thought of it. That too was instantly forgiven."

"My brother says something that is impossible to believe."

"You must believe it; I proved long ago that it was forgiven, for if it were not I should have revenged myself on your father. Do you suppose that Old Shatterhand could be treated thus, and not reply with his fist if he resented it?"

"We wondered afterward that you did not do this."

"The father of Winnetou cannot insult me. It was all a mistake; that is all. Let us talk of something else."

"I must speak of this, for I should be guilty if I did not tell my brother the custom of our people. No brave ever admits a mistake, and a chief can do so least of all. Intschu-Tschuna knows that he did wrong, but he cannot ask your forgiveness. Therefore he bade me speak of it to you. Winnetou acts for his father."

"That was not at all necessary, and in any case we are quits, for I insulted you."

"Never."

"Yes. Isn't a blow of the fist an insult?"

"That was in combat, where it cannot count as an insult. My brother is noble and generous; we will not forget it in him."

"Let us speak of other things, dear Winnetou. I am to become an Apache; how will it be with my comrades?"

"They cannot be taken into the tribe, but they are our brothers."

"Without any ceremony?"

"To-morrow we will smoke the pipe of peace with them. In my white brother's home in the rising sun is there no calumet?"

"No; Christians are all brothers, and it is not necessary to announce it."

"All brothers! Is there no strife between them?"

"Certainly there is."

"Then they are not different from us, or better than we. They teach love, but do not feel it. Why did my brother come here?"

The Indians never ask such personal questions; but Winnetou could do so in my case, because we were to be brothers, and he must learn to know me.

"I wanted to see the West, and I wanted to try my skill in my profession, and above all I wanted to win honor."

"I do not see how you could win honor by—" He paused.

"By stealing your lands," I finished for him. "Truly, Winnetou, I never thought of that side at all. I was not to profit by the road, except as I did my work well, and was paid for it."

"Paid! paid! Do you care for gold? Do you need it?"

"I have an uncle, a second father, who will give me all I require; but every young man of spirit wants to make his own name and fortune."

"And measuring for that road would have done this?"

"It would have been a first step, and a long one, towards it."

"And now you will not get your reward, because the measuring is not done?"

"No."

"How much longer time would have been necessary to finish it?"

"Only one day."

"Had I known you as I know you now we would have delayed a day in coming back."

"That I might have finished my work?" I asked, touched by such generosity.

"Yes."

"That means that you would have consented to the robbery."

"Not to the robbery, but only to the measuring. The lines you make on paper do us no harm; the robbery only begins when the laborers of the pale-faces come to build the road for their fire-horse."

He considered a while, and a thought was shaping in his brain of such nobility that I doubt if many white men would have been capable of entertaining it. At last he uttered it: "My white brother shall receive all the instruments again, and I will ask my father to allow him to finish measuring for the road. We will go with our warriors and protect him while he does this, and he shall send his papers to the men who wanted them, as well as their instruments, and so shall he make this first step towards the name and fortune he desires."

"Winnetou," I cried, moved beyond expression by a generosity which I could hardly fathom, "dear, noble, kind Winnetou, there is no one like you. I can never thank you."

"There can never be thanks due me from you; my debt must always be greater than yours, and my father has said we shall be as one man with two bodies. But how are you to use this name and fortune? Not here among the Apaches. Will you then go away from us?"

"Yes, but not immediately."

"We shall be sorrowful. You are to be given the power and rank of a chief of the Apaches. We believed you would stay with us always, even as Kleki-Petrah stayed to the day of his death."

"My circumstances are very different from his."

"You are to become Winnetou's brother, according to Kleki-Petrah's will, yet you would forsake him. Is that right?"

"Yes; for brothers cannot be constantly together when they have different duties to fulfil. I must go back to those who love me at home, and to whom I owe so much, and see them as well as my other brother here."

"Then we shall see you again?"

"Of course you will, for my heart will draw me back to you."

"That rejoices my soul. Whenever you come we shall be glad. You speak of other duties and other friends. Could you not be happy with us?"

"Honestly, I don't know. I love Winnetou, and admire his noble father; but I have been here too short a time to answer that question. It is as when two birds alight on the branch of a tree. One is nourished by the fruit of that tree; the other requires different food, and must fly away."

"Yet you must believe that we would give you everything you desire."

"Indeed I know it; but when I spoke of food, I did not mean the nourishment of the body."

"Yes, I understand; you pale-faces speak of a food of the soul. I have heard of it from Kleki-Petrah. He missed this food among us, and sometimes he was very sad, though he tried not to let us see it. But every spring he journeyed to Santa Fé, and was refreshed in soul. So, if my dear brother Jack must go, he shall go; but his red brother begs him to come back again."

This was the first time Winnetou had ever called me by my own name, and I was more than surprised to discover in him a knowledge of the most sacred of Catholic practices, for of course he spoke of Kleki-Petrah's going to Santa Fé to fulfil his Easter duties.

"Winnetou," I answered sincerely, "whatever there is at home that I love—and there is much,—and whatever there is in the great cities of the East to satisfy mind and soul, believe me I have learned to love you and respect you too deeply to leave you willingly; and if I go away, nothing but death shall keep me from returning to my red brother's side. And some day my brave Winnetou's noble soul also shall be nourished with that heavenly Food which Kleki-Petrah went so far to seek, and which I need to help me on the way he has gone."

"You are then a Christian, really believing in your faith?" he asked.

"I don't say I'm a good Christian,—God alone knows whether or not I am that,—but I have strong faith; yes, and I'd gladly be a good one."

"And you think we are heathen?"

"No; you believe in the great, Good Spirit, and never worship idols."

"Then grant me one request."

"Gladly. What is it?"

"Never speak of your faith to me. Never try to convert me. It is as Kleki-Petrah said. Your faith may be the true one, but we red men cannot understand it. If Christians did not drive us out and oppress us, we might feel that they were good men, and hold their teaching as good. Then we might have time and place to learn what one needs to know of your Holy Book and your priests' teaching in order to understand them. But he who is slowly and surely driven to death cannot feel that the religion of those who kill him is the religion of love."

"You must distinguish between the religion and the followers who only acknowledge it in words, but never act by its light," I said, at a loss how to meet this reproach.

"So all the pale-faces say. Men call themselves Christians, yet do not act as such. I cannot understand how it is that only one man, and now that you have come I will say two men, of all the pale-faces I have known, lived up to the Christian belief. We have our good Manitou, who wishes all men to be good. I try to do as He wishes. Perhaps I am a Christian—a better one than those who are so particular about the name, but have no love in them, and never follow Christian teachings. So never speak to me of your faith, and never try to make me a man who is called a Christian, yet may be none. That is the request you must fulfil."

I gave the promise, and have kept it. Are words necessary? Is not practice a more eloquent preacher than mere speech? "By their fruits ye shall know them," said Our Lord; and I vowed in my heart to be Winnetou's teacher by my life. There came an evening at last, never to be forgotten, when he spoke on this subject himself, and in bitter pain I reaped the fruit of loving prayer and patient sowing as the dearest friend I ever had lay dead with the waters of baptism glistening on his brow.

Now I contented myself with a pressure of his hand, signifying that I understood all the bitterness the wrongs of his race caused him, and we said no more. Presently we arose, for the sun had gone down in splendor, and the river was growing purple as the light faded. We went back to the pueblo, and the brave chief, who was looking for us, welcomed us with a fatherly kindness I had not felt in him before. We sat down to our smoking meal together, and the beautiful Fair Day served us so gracefully, so affectionately, that I thought with wonder how truly among all sorts of men home was home, and love made home-coming sweet.

CHAPTER XIX.

THE BURIAL OF KLEKI-PETRAH.

The morning dawned fair and warm, and the pueblo was early astir for the burial of Kleki-Petrah. Not all of the Apaches lived in the pueblo, for though it was large it would have been far too small to have accommodated them. Only Intschu-Tschuna and his most important braves dwelt here, forming with their families and herds of horses the central point of the tribe of Mascaleros-Apaches. From this pueblo the chief ruled over the tribe, and thence took long journeys to the various branches of the great Apache family which acknowledged him as their head.

Representatives of every tribe had assembled to pay their last tribute to the white friend whom they had all loved and honored, and who had been faithful to them even unto death.

We, my comrades and I, repaired early to the spot where the grave was to be erected. I estimated the height and breadth of the mass of stone, and then, taking a tomahawk, Hawkins, Stone, Parker, and I went through the woods, following the river downward, seeking a suitable tree from which to make a cross.

When we returned to the burial-place the sorrowful ceremonies had begun. The Indians had worked

THE BURIAL OF KLEKI-PETRAH. 215

rapidly on the construction of the tomb, which was nearly finished. It was surrounded by braves, who were intoning their peculiar and profoundly touching death-song. Its dull, monotonous tone was broken occasionally by a shrill, piercing cry, which startled the ear as a sudden flash of lightning from heavy clouds startles the eye by flashing across it. Twelve Indians were working on the tomb under the direction of the two chiefs, and between them and the singers danced a figure decked in all the insignia of his race, and making grotesque, slow motions, and curious leaps.

"Who is that—the medicine-man?" I asked.

"Yes," Sam replied.

"Indian customs at the burial of a Catholic! What do you say to that, my dear Sam?"

"You don't like it?" asked Sam.

"Certainly not."

"Then don't show it. You would offend the Apaches mortally."

"But this absurd mumming annoys me more than I can say."

"They mean well; they can't do better than they know. It isn't heathenish. These good folks believe in one Great Spirit, to whom their dead friend and teacher has gone. They bid him farewell, and mourn his death in their own way, and everything that medicine-man does has a symbolic meaning. Let them do as they will. There is no priest anywhere near here, and they won't prevent us putting our cross at the head of the grave."

As we placed the cross before the coffin Winnetou

asked: "Shall this sign of Christianity be placed over the grave?"

"Yes."

"That is right. I should have asked my brother Old Shatterhand to make a cross, for Kleki-Petrah had one in his dwelling, and begged us to put one over his grave when he should die. Where must it stand?"

"At the head of the grave."

"As in those great, tall houses in which Christians pray to the Great Spirit? I have seen them. It shall be as you wish. Sit here and see that it is done properly."

In a short time the tomb was complete; it was crowned by our cross, and had an opening left to receive the coffin, which still stood outside. Then came Nscho-Tschi. She had been to the pueblo to get two clay cups, which she had taken to the river and filled with water. Having done this she returned to the grave and set them on the coffin—for what purpose I was soon to learn.

Everything was now ready for the burial. Intschu-Tschuna gave a signal with his hand for the song of lamentation to cease. The medicine-man squatted upon the ground. The chief went up to the coffin, and spoke, slowly and solemnly. "My brothers and sisters of all the tribes of the Apaches," he began, "the sun rises in the morning in the east and sinks at night into the west, and the year awakes in the spring-time and in winter sleeps again. So is it also with man. Is this true?"

"How!" arose heavily on all sides.

"Man rises like the sun, and sinks again into the

grave. He comes like spring upon the earth, and like winter lays himself down to rest. But though the sun sets, it shines again in the morning; and when winter disappears, once more the spring is here. Is this true ?"

"How!"

"Thus has Kleki-Petrah taught us. Man will be laid in the grave, but beyond death he rises again, like a new day and a new spring, to live forever in the land of the great Good Spirit. This has Kleki-Petrah told us; and now he knows whether he spoke truly or not, for he has disappeared like the day and the year, and his spirit has gone to the dwelling of the dead, for which he always longed. Is this true ?"

"How!"

"His faith was not ours, nor is our faith his. We hate our enemies and love our friends; but he taught us that man must also love his enemies, for they too are our brothers. That we do not believe; yet when we have obeyed his words it has been peaceful and well for us. Perhaps his faith is also ours, only we could not understand him as he wished to be understood. We say our spirits go to the eternal Happy Hunting Grounds, and he hoped for eternal Blessedness. Often I think our Hunting Grounds may be his Blessedness. Is this true ?"

"How!"

"He often told us of the Saviour who came to make all men blessed. We believe in his words, because there was never a lie on his lips. This Saviour came for all men; has He been with the red man ? If He came, we would welcome Him; for we shall be destroyed or driven away by the pale-faces, and we long for Him. Is this true?"

"How!"

"This was Kleki-Petrah's teaching. Now I speak of his end. It came upon him as a wild beast falls upon its prey. Sudden and unforeseen it was. He was strong and well, and stood at our side. He would have mounted his horse and ridden home with us, but the bullet of the murderer struck him. My brothers and sisters may lament him."

There arose a dull cry of woe, growing louder and higher, till it ended in a piercing shriek. Then the chief continued: "We have avenged his death. The cowardly dog who killed him was not worthy to follow him in death; he has been shot by the children, and his body floats down the stream. Is this true?"

"How!"

"Now is the spirit of Kleki-Petrah gone from us, but his body remains, over which we raise a memorial to him, to show to our successors that we had a good White Father who was our teacher, and whom we loved. He was not born in this land, but he came from afar, beyond the big water, where oaks grow. So to honor him and speak of our love for him we have brought an oak to plant beside his grave. And as it sprouts and spreads so will his spirit grow great beyond the grave. And as the oak grows so will the words which we have heard from him sprout in our hearts, and our spirits shall find shelter under its shade. But he has not gone from us without sending us a pale-face who shall be our friend and brother in his place. Here you see Old Shatterhand, a white man who knows all that Kleki-Petrah knew, and is a stronger warrior than he. He has killed the grizzly bear with his knife, and all his foes he strikes to earth with his fist. Intschu-Tschuna and Winnetou were repeatedly in his power, yet he did not slay us, but gave us our lives, because he loved us, and is a friend of the red man. Is this true?"

"How!"

"It was Kleki-Petrah's last word and last wish that Old Shatterhand should be his successor with the Apache warriors, and Old Shatterhand has promised to fulfil this wish. Therefore he shall be received into the Apache tribe and become a chief. It shall be as though he were red of skin, and born among us. To accomplish this he must have smoked the calumet with every grown warrior of the Apaches; but this shall not be necessary, for he will drink Winnetou's blood, and Winnetou will drink his, and then he will be blood of our blood, and flesh of our flesh. Do the Apache braves agree to this?"

"How! how! how!" arose, thrice repeated, the unanimous response of all present.

"Then let Winnetou and Old Shatterhand come here to the coffin, and let their blood drop into the water of the bond of brotherhood."

I had often read of the blood bond of brotherhood. It is a custom among many savage and half-civilized people, and usually consists of the mingling of the blood of the two making the compact, which is drunk by both, and in consequence they become more closely united, more truly brothers, than if they had been born of the same parents.

Winnetou and I were to drink each other's blood. We placed ourselves on each side of the coffin, and Intschu-Tschuna pricked first his son's wrist, holding it over the cup which Nscho-Tschi had brought. A tiny drop of blood fell into it, and the chief set it aside. Then he repeated the proceeding with me, and a tiny drop of my blood fell into the other cup. Winnetou took the cup containing my blood in his hand, and I received the one with his. Then Intschu-Tschuna said: "Life dwells in the blood. The souls of these two young men shall mingle till there is but one soul in them. Old Shatterhand's thoughts shall be Winnetou's thoughts, and what Winnetou wills that shall also be the will of Old Shatterhand. Drink!" I raised my cup as Winnetou raised his. It was Rio Pecos water, to which the single drop of blood in it imparted no taste. As we set down the empty cups the chief took my hand and said: "Thou art now the son of my flesh equally with Winnetou, and a warrior of our people. The renown of thy deeds shall be quickly known everywhere, and no other warrior shall surpass thee. Thou art a chief of the Apaches, and all branches of our people shall honor thee as such."

This was indeed rapid advancement—from a young, newly graduated collegiate to a chief of the Apaches; and I could not help fancying the faces of my friends at home if they could see me now. And yet, strange and wild as was the life around me, these fine red men were far more congenial to me than many of my former associates.

How completely the words of Intschu-Tschuna were fulfilled that Winnetou and I should be but one soul in two bodies! We grew to understand each other without a word; we had but to look at each other to know what we desired and felt, and there was never the slightest disagreement between us. But I suspect this was less because we had drunk one another's blood than because there was naturally a strong attraction and sympathy between us; and never again shall I love another friend as I loved my brave Apache brother, my true-hearted Winnetou!

As Intschu-Tschuna spoke the last words all the Apaches had risen, even the children, to shout a loud, applauding "How!" Then the chief added: "Now is the new, the living Kleki-Petrah received among us, and we can lay the dead in his grave. My brothers may now do this." This was spoken to the Indians who had built the tomb. I asked for a few minutes' delay, and nodded to Sam Hawkins, Dick Stone, and Will Parker to come up; with these standing by me I said an *Our Father*, a *Hail Mary*, and a *De Profundis* over the coffin. Then was the body of the former atheist and revolutionist, and at last the penitent and missionary, lowered into the middle of the tomb, which the Indians sealed to await the dawn of that new day of which Intschu-Tschuna had spoken.

This was my first experience of a burial ceremony among savages, and it deeply impressed me. I was touched by the half perception of truth which appeared in the chief's words. Especially was I moved by the longing for the coming of one who was to deliver them, which rang in these words,—a longing like that of the people of Israel as they waited for the Messias.

While the grave was closing the Indians' death-chant was sung again, and it sank into silence when the last stone was placed; the Apaches rose from their places, and the whole great assembly seemed to melt away in the stillness broken only by the fall of their moccasins, the rustling of the leaves, and the ripple of the Rio Pecos. Nscho-Tschi came from among the women and stood at her father's right hand, Winnetou's arm lay across my shoulders as he stood at his father's other side, and Intschu-Tschuna had taken my right hand in his own. "You are my children, and I am happy in you," he said. "I thank the Great Spirit that He has protected me through danger, and given me a strong, brave, faithful son, and my other children a brother to protect them when I am gone."

"No, Intschu-Tschuna," I said. "Rather should I thank Him for the love and kindness I find so far from home, and among a strange people."

"They are your people now," said Nscho-Tschi quickly.

"And we are all happy and blest in one another," said Winnetou. "All grateful for the happy ending of a story begun in sorrow and wrath. Come, my brother; let us go to the dwelling of our father Intschu-Tschuna. A new life has begun for us all to-day."

And so we walked together to the great pueblo, silent

and peaceful, though saddened by the solemn ceremony and parting from one the three Indians had loved so well.

Winnetou spoke truly: though the story of our meeting ended here, a new life had indeed begun; and unconscious of what lay before us we went home together, turning our backs on what had been, and setting our faces towards the future.

www.ingramcontent.com/pod-product-compliance
Lightning Source LLC
Chambersburg PA
CBHW031820230426
43669CB00009B/1206